T0328559

DIALECTICAL
THINKING

DIALECTICAL THINKING

ZENO, SOCRATES, KANT, AND MARX

Tommi Juhani Hanhijärvi

Algora Publishing
New York

Library of Congress Cataloging-in-Publication Data —

Hanhijärvi, Tommi Juhani.
   Dialectical thinking : Zeno, Socrates, Kant, Marx / Tommi Juhani Hanhijdrvi.
      pages cm
   Includes bibliographical references and index.
   ISBN 978-1-62894-123-4 (soft cover : alk. paper) — ISBN 978-1-62894-124-1 (hard
cover: alk. paper) — ISBN 978-1-62894-125-8 (ebook) 1. Thought and thinking. 2.
Philosophy. 3. Reasoning. 4. Dialectical materialism. 5. Zeno, of Elea. 6. Socrates. 7. Kant,
Immanuel, 1724-1804. 8. Marx, Karl, 1818-1883. I. Title.
   B105.T54H36 2015
   190—dc23
                                2015009449

Printed in the United States

Table of Contents

This book grew out of my experiences as a philosophy teacher in the past few years, most recently at the University of Helsinki. My students often asked me for explanations that were missing from the books that I was able to find. I felt I had to invent the answers myself. But then, curiously, the answers I invented seemed to work. How? First, the students normally understood them easily. Second, many students found them useful in formulating their own arguments. Third, the original texts of philosophy that we read, from Hinduism, Plato, and Aristotle, to Aquinas, Descartes, Kant, and so on, seemed often to accord with the patterns I articulated. It appeared, therefore, that the gap had been filled. But in this way the materials for a new book had simultaneously been created. Much of the material of this book is material from the classes I have taught. I am now telling a wider audience of readers quite nearly what I have already told a smaller group of students in person.

I should point out, however, that my students' questions did not concern only the word or concept of "dialectic." They had no reason to focus so much on that. Rather the issue was often what type of reasoning *philosophers* tend to use. How was one to read a passage in Plato, or in Descartes? What kind of a thing was aspired to in philosophy in the first place? Why should one philosophize? What was this thing called "philosophy" about on a general level anyway? It is not science, obviously, but nor is it only myth. I felt that there was a need to identify a generalized kind or type of *reasoning* that could be called uniquely philosophical, for in this way the students could be expected to respect the sources that we examined. Accordingly, my first formulations of the dialectical pattern concerned philosophical reasoning in general.

How did the recent philosophy books *fall short* of the needs of my classes? Reasoning in so many recent textbooks, and also in so many recent scholarly works in my experience, is presented only as something deductive or inductive (or at most abductive). This makes the resources of reasoning too poor. The generative potentials are gone. The drama is missing. Where are the big questions about the foundations of knowledge, about first causes, about final aims, etc.? Are not such big questions somehow reasonable? And how about the big answers, that is the "deep" theories which present us with a Form or an Idea, an unmoved mover, a *Cogito*, a *Geist*, a labor power? Is there no rational vocabulary for them? Are so many classics to appear only as something strange and archaic? This could not be accepted. The ambitious philosophies have a force of their own and this force needs to be recognized.

It could have been, of course, that recent works on *dialectics* in particular would have provided us with satisfactory models for reasoning. But the sad truth is that usually the recent books on dialectics are too loose. For example, if some Platonists have said that dialectic is about questioning and answering then that is too loose because a conversation about what you did last summer, for example, is not dialectical. It is not a piece of reasoning, and it is not something philosophical. The situation is not much improved if the answers must be definitions, because a definition is as such nothing philosophical yet. One may define water as a chemical compound and do no philosophy at all. A Platonic dialectic is something *more* than this. So is a Hegelian dialectic. It is not informative to hear of triplets of theses–antitheses–syntheses if no one can clearly and briefly explain syntheses (or *aufheben*, etc.). For how is a "synthesis" something self-conscious or conceptual as Hegel intends? The *word* "synthesis" does not tell one this. But nor is it helpful to say, with e.g. Engels (see Chapter 4 below), that dialectics simply *lack* any general features. For then there is no generalized manner of reasoning at all. Then there are only anomalous details. Yet if philosophy is only a lot of anomalous details then I am not sure why students should learn it, or indeed why I should teach it.

I need to admit that I got no one's *permission* to invent a dialectical pattern and to use it in my teaching. The risk is my own. Maybe one day I will be caught for having taught my own fictions as deep truths to hundreds or even thousands of people. Of course that would be a sin, and I would then need to regret my behavior. But it could also turn out, as I think I am still entitled to believe, that in the future my innovations are revealed as only modest copies of dialectics proper, whether those proper originals are hidden in the past or in the future. This would be the optimal result for me. I would then be a mere gateway to a thing that transcends my own bounds. Of course, only time will tell which way matters actually turn out, and for now all I can do is spread the word.

TJH, March 2015

INTRODUCTION

> The world wouldn't exist if it didn't have the power to lib-
> erate itself.
>
> — Jack Kerouac

Do you tend to view both sides of an issue, not taking either side with confidence until you absolutely must?

Do you enjoy ironies and paradoxes, and like to point out how things fit or do not fit with themselves?

Are you disturbed, or inspired or otherwise touched, by the oddity that sometimes nothing in life or the universe seems absolutely central, or that everything seems somehow conditional and optional, like a game of sorts?

If you have answered at least one of these questions with *Yes* then you may have opened the right book. For you have now been identified as a natural *dialectician.*

Dialectical thinking goes back to ancient times, but it also has major modern representatives. This book concentrates on the thought of

Zeno (Elea, Greece, ca. 490 B.C.E.–430 B.C.E.), who invented paradoxes like that of Achilles and the tortoise. His riddles challenge the best minds to this day.

Socrates (Athens, Greece, ca. 469–399 B.C.E.), who came up with some of the deepest categories for self-scrutiny and social criticism. These have been enormously influential in the history of Western philosophy.

Immanuel Kant (Königsberg, Germany, 1724–1804), whose *Critique of Pure Reason* exposes the contradictions of the most basic metaphysical reflections. He is often viewed as the greatest modern philosopher.

Karl Marx (Germany, France, and the UK, 1818–1883), who said that we all yearn for self-expression but tend to hide behind gods, conventional authorities, and material products. Marx is perhaps the most influential social theorist in modern history.

In this book these four heroes of dialectics are discussed: Zeno, Socrates, Kant, and Marx. Each of them applies dialectic to an area of life to which he thinks it is fitted. In Socrates and Marx there is a concern with values, whether religious, moral, or legal. Zeno and Kant use dialectic to study fundamental aspects of reality. So dialectic is sometimes about how one ought to live, and other times it is more about how the universe is. Arguably some of the major intellectual achievements of our species may be credited to dialectic.

In this book the historical contexts of these thinkers will be briefly outlined; their thought is analyzed at length; and special emphasis is given to the current and future uses of dialectics. For the dialecticians of the past provide us, too, with tools for critical thought. Learning more about them may actually be a liberating experience.

What *is* dialectical thinking? Let us begin with some intuitions.

Dialectic is, for one thing, thinking in oppositions, conflicts, or contraries. In this vein, the great dialecticians of the past have been concerned with problems and disturbing issues. It has never been the choice of the dialectician to take the easy way out. A dialectician is more like an intellectual trouble-maker. She is lively, disquieting, always pushing further at the ultimate frontiers.

A second main aspect of dialectic is its self-concern. A dialectician is always concerned with some *locus* of thought. This may be the thought of whoever she happens to be speaking with. Or it may be her own. Again, it may be thought or reasoning in the abstract, as an ideal of perfect, "divine," thinking. In any case the problems the dialectician deals in are not about, say, stars or germs. They are about our very own operations: our evaluations, criticisms, plans, even memories, etc.

Originally in ancient Greece "dialectic" (διαλεκτική) meant "skill in talking," but because of its philosophical uses it came to mean something more like problem-solving. It is not flowery like rhetoric, but nor is it mechanical like logic.

Thought of this general sort has been instanced also in ancient Asian cultures, at least in the Hinduist *Vedas* and *Upanishads* and the Daoist *Tao Te Ching*, and some of their examples may precede the Greek ones.[1]

Now let us move from intuitions to structures and define dialectic. There are relations, like:

---

[1] Zaehner introduces readers to Hinduism and Hansen to Daoism.

eats. This is for example between a cat and a mouse and between a mouse and a piece of cheese. So one might write: cat eats mouse eats cheese or, if eats = R1, aR1bR1c. Notice that cat ≠ mouse ≠ cheese though R1 is constantly the same. R1 repeats and repeats though the terms (a, b, c) do not. So one relation binds together different things. In a long food chain, the terms run all the way from a to z.

teaches (R2). I am teaching you, in a way, and you may teach someone else. But I was also taught by someone, who was taught by someone else, etc. And the individuals you teach may teach others. So the same line continues at both ends. R2 does not begin or end in this book.

Here are some relations that have typically interested philosophers:

is a means to (R3). Now, a is a means to further means and z is the ultimate aim. E.g., matches (= a) to fire (= b) to heat (= c) to melting metals (= d) to making tools (= e), etc.

effects (R4). The first event in history is a and the last is z. So on the left, we have *Genesis* or the Big Bang and on the right the apocalypse.

is a physical part of (R5). The entire universe is z and its smallest element is a. So this R gradually zooms out, from the microscopic to the telescopic.

has the form (R6). Now there is more and more order as one moves towards the right, so a is nearly chaotic and z is as structured as it is possible to be.[1]

Now we can already say what the great dialecticians do. Their

- *questions* (issues, problems, mysteries) are whether some R or other begins or ends somewhere or not. So there is or is not a final aim, a first cause, a smallest part, a greatest whole, a meta-model, etc. So this is the kind of thing that one often philosophizes *about* in dialectics.
- *answers* (solutions, theories) are self-relational, taking some R as a term. Thus Plato's Ideas (Forms), Aristotle's God, Descartes' *Cogito*, Hegel's *Geist*, the Hindu *Atman*, etc. So

---

[1] "R3," "R4," "R5," and "R6" are not the symbols that dialecticians have normally used. For example Aristotle, philosophizing in ancient Greece, calls these relations by the following names:
R3 = final cause.
R4 = efficient cause.
R5 = material cause.
R6 = formal cause.
These are far from being the only relations that dialecticians have operated with. Also, all dialecticians do not care for all relations. For instance Plato, also in ancient Greece, often focuses on the likes of R3 and R6 and cares little for R5. There are many different philosophers and theologians using this same form. They are all "dialecticians."

the ultimate problems are supposedly solved by reference to self-motion, self-consciousness, self-knowledge, etc. This is the kind of *claim* one often finds in the great dialectical philosophies.

So what makes a dialectician? Posing extreme questions and giving self-relational answers.

Now the reader knows.

What the rest of this book will do is look at different versions of dialectics and find out what can be done with them. On the one hand we will find out what *has been done* with them and on the other we will try to reveal what is *yet to be done*. All or most riddles in this region have not been solved. There is space for future pioneers! They may come.

But before we go into that we need to clarify some things.

A first thing that may need explaining is how dialectical *questions arise*. Why must questions ever get extreme? Where does the pressure come from that takes us all the way to the ultimate issues? Is it not rational to be more moderate?

Consider this anecdote first:

> "The world, marm," said I, anxious to display my acquired knowledge, "is not exactly round, but resembles in shape a flattened orange; and it turns on its axis once in twenty-four hours."
>
> "Well, I don't know anything about its *axes*," replied she, "but I know it don't turn round, for if it did we'd be all tumbled off; and as to its being round, anyone can see it's a square piece of ground, standing on a rock!"
>
> "Standing on a rock! but upon what does that stand?"
>
> "Why, on another, to be sure!"
>
> "But what supports the last?"
>
> "Lud! child, how stupid you are! There's rocks all the way down!

The narrator maintains a scientific worldview but the other speaker says that the earth is placed on a rock. When asked what the rock is placed on, she answers, "another rock." Thus there is a relation, is placed on, which is between several objects: the earth, a rock, a further rock, yet a further rock, etc. These objects we may symbolize with a, b, c, d, etc. The relation we can call R7, to distinguish it from eats and the others above. The structure we get is: aR7bR7cR7d...[1]

---

[1] The "..." at the end means that the series is endless or else that it does not matter for now how it may end. The special symbols "R" and "a" repeat because this way it is more obvious that the same pattern repeats, as with eats (the eater is eaten). We get formally or structurally

This is the same structure as before. But unlike with eats we now have a dramatic question: Does the pile of rocks have an ultimate basis somewhere, or is it rocks all the way down? That is, is the series of rocks finite or infinite? This is a typical issue for dialectics. The *need* of final points is more urgent with R7 than with eats. That is why I brought up R7. R7 shows why extreme questions can arise.

Is this clear?

Consider another anecdote:

> Jim, 5, and I were walking in Helsinki and came across a street musician, who played melodies by hitting bottles (with spoons, I think). He was very skilled and had a large audience and several children got to drop a coin or two into his little box. Jim also got to do this. But soon he was lost in thought.
>
> Why does the musician need money? he asked me.
>
> He needs to buy food, and clothes, and to pay the rent, etc., I explained. So many things cost money. One needs money to ride a tram, to get a toothbrush, everything. The bottle player is poor so he has to play on the street to get his money.
>
> It had not occurred to little Jim that so many things have a price tag on them. After a minute of silence he asked:
>
> ...Where does the bottle player get his bottles, then?

I argued that he could find *those*. But obviously it would be hard to get started with earning *anything* if *everything* had a price tag on it, so Jim's question was well founded.

Instead of is placed on or eats, we now have demands as our relation: a demands b demands c demands d. Paying the rent demands money demands playing bottles demands bottles to start with; d is the bedrock in this series. Little Jim's wonder was aroused by the question whether there *is* a bedrock. I assured him that there is. This issue between us was exactly about the extreme. I think everyone can understand now how the issue about final limits can arise quite easily, if one thinks about things.

Consider yet a third anecdote to see how a dialectic *terminates:*

---

dialectical strings or chains with many different contents or characters. (It is as with 1+1 = 2. You can add two apples together or two oranges: the formula for adding is the same. I am saying that there is a *formula* for dialectics, not only for, e.g., elementary arithmetic. That there is a dialectical formula is the thesis of this book.)
On the logic of relations see Russell, *The Principles of Mathematics*, pp. 23-26 and 49-52. (Russell is no dialectician. But like so many others he could sometimes be interpreted in dialectical terms. Relational logic is one opportunity for doing this, and "Russell's Paradox" is another. Russell's Paradox concerns the set of all sets, and it is self-relational.)

Father: Good morning, child, it is time to get up!

Child: ...Why?

Father: Dear, you need to go to school.

Child: What for, Daddy?

Father: So that you will learn so many things.

Child: And why?

Father: Child, it is for your own good. You will learn to think.

Child: Why Daddy?

Father: You will learn to think for yourself about how to think, and that is an end in itself.

The child may not get out of bed with this but the self-relational termination is dialectical. It uses a relation (basically R3, from above) repeatedly to make a question more and more intense and then finally it self-applies that relation to build a conclusion.

If thought about thought is indeed a means to itself then that *is* the endpoint. It is even if the child does not understand.

Why is it, though? The reason is simple: the end is a circle. It contains its own why. If you ask why, in this circle, then it will just spin you around. All the earlier why's passed the buck, but this one keeps piling it on itself. The circle will just repeat, like a spinning wheel, if the child still keeps asking.

One could have a dialectical termination also by letting the *child* win. She would win if she asked why she asks why (as did my childhood friend of four). She would still be after an answer from her father, because she would still be raising a question. But she would have already come to the high point of the conversation. How so? Well, she could not advance any further in the same direction anymore. If she asked why she asks why she asks why, then the drama would already be gone. That question would be only "academic" if she had already found an answer to why she asks why. Put differently, the second order is as high as one needs to go with this relation. If you go further up, you will not get anything more interesting.

But one must be careful. It is not quite a generalizable rule that a second order is as high as you need to rise. Some relations *do* operate well even if you pursue them to higher orders. Witness this one:

- **means** (R8). A dark cloud means rain, and crying means pain, but what does "means" mean? If we answer this, we get "means" means A, but we can continue unpacking our answer (that is A) with AAB, and from here we can go on to BBC,

CCD, etc., without end. That is, we do not have to reach a bedrock for the relation (= R8) to apply without end. The orders can keep getting higher.

Why is this? The reason is simple: R8 is a *productive* relation. It changes, even replaces, what it concerns. This opens up the opportunity for a brand new question. (For you can ask about A what it A's, and then about B what it B's, etc. You do not repeat the question because the topics change with every answer.)

In what way is R8 productive? A in the above cannot spell "means," because to say that " 'Means' means 'means' " is illogical. Why is it illogical? Well, if you explain the meaning of something, then you are supposed to say something *more* meaningful about it than what you began with. You need to *advance* in meaningfulness as you go down the line. What R8 requires is that you keep giving more and more meaningful symbols as time passes. That is how R8 is a productive relation. You just cannot keep repeating yourself if you use it. It forces you do advance — or else you are just not using it.

And why is this? How can a relation like meaning, or any relation, have a character of its own in this way? How can a relation force us into anything? It follows simply from the content of the relation. The situation is no different, in principle, than how "sits on" requires, as its term or object, something one can sit on. I cannot sit on a memory, a state, etc. There is a range of things to which the relation applies: stools, rooftops, etc. That is how *all* relations are: all of them have their requirements. To the right of "splits into" you have double the number of things that you have to its left. If you do not, then "splits into" is not what happens. The environment comes with the relation.

Now we move on to the next preliminary clarification.

There is no *specific class* of questions for generating dialectics. One cannot always just ask *Why?*, for example, because it will not make sense in response to everything. What matters is not so much which question you need as how far you go with it. The questions we use in dialectics can be *Why?* or *What is...?* or *Where is...?*, etc., but the recipe for forming dialectics is normally to repeat the same question until you can no longer do so.

But also, there is no necessity to use *questions* in *all* dialectics. Even if a child asks nothing from anybody and simply forms a complete relational series on her own, in her thoughts, then nonetheless she is a dialectician, then and there. No one needs to hear about it for it to happen. All dialectics are not dialogical. They can be "monological." It is perfectly permissible for a dialectician to meditate alone.

On the other hand, there is no necessity to work alone *either*. One has a dialectic as soon as one has the above structure: aRbRc...zRz or ... zRR (or else aRa... or RRa...). It is as simple as that. Whatever *way* you do it is inessential.

In the same spirit, it is perfectly allowed to use exotic codes. And there is also no requirement regarding time. Perhaps one can form one's series in a second, or maybe it will take a decade — no matter. One can be spontaneous or plan, etc. (Can one do dialectics in music? I do not know.)

At the center of every dialectic is a *self*. What is a "self"?

The self in a dialectic is something that relates to itself. To be a self, or to have a self, is the same thing as relating to oneself (for instance by teaching oneself or moving oneself).

A dialectical self is peculiar in the way that it is not something you can see in the mirror. Rather, the self is a *relation* to things. Roughly the self is a *thinker* in Socrates, a *chooser* in Kant, and a *creator* in Marx. The self makes its appearance in its relationships, that is in the ways that it contacts objects. It may alter objects or select between them. At any rate it leaves its mark, and from that mark it sees itself.

But then there is the self-relational twist to this. In Socrates one thinks *about* thought, and evolves from metaphors and myths about it to contradictions and finally to definitions. In the final stage one knows oneself, and is free. In Kant one chooses to choose, taking responsibility. In Marx one produces tools for production, somewhat like cave dwellers produced an axe. One not only uses tools, but makes them. In general, the dialectical self is not *only* a relation, or a *normal* relation. The dialectical self is a relation *to a* relation, a relation which alters itself.

A humorous version of this would be that of Baron Münchhausen, who lifts himself in the air by the hair. He does something impossible, to be sure, and often dialectical selves are not impossible at all. But the idea in a dialectic is always to use a relation to get above or beyond that same relation, and this is similar to lifting oneself by the hair. It is to move without any external foothold. It is to have movement on a purely internal basis. This will be clearer once we come to actually consider the philosophies of Socrates, Kant, and Marx.

Who has normally used dialectics? Is there a generalization about what kinds of people go for them? Are there professions in this area? Do dialecticians have a particular reputation?

I have mentioned major philosophers and theologians from the East and the West. Three major topics for dialecticians have been:

- *Freedom.* Can you see why? If dialectical arguments target at self-relations then that is not so far from saying that they target at whatever is self-sufficient, self-ruled, self-made — that is, free. But this is freedom in what is called a "positive" sense, not in a "negative" one. Negative liberty means that you are *not* ruled by *other* agents. Positive liberty means that you are ruled by yourself. Liberal constitutions, like the American and the French and so many others these days, guarantee negative liberties. These are weaker than positive ones because even if you are negatively free you may not be positively: I may leave you alone, and everyone may leave you alone, but that does not yet mean that you make anything of yourself. You are negatively free also in sleeping and day-dreaming! In being positively free you cannot do that, for more is required. You need to cultivate yourself or you are *not* free, positively. Dialectics are instrumental to positive liberty, not to negative liberty.

- *Knowledge.* Skeptics doubt that knowledge is possible in one area of life or another. The typical skeptical dialectic consists of a repeated question, addressed to someone who claims to know: *How do you know a? What is your proof?* If the answer is b, the next skeptical question is, *How do you prove b?* Then one needs c, etc., and a series is formed in dialectical spirit. Now, if the answerer succeeds in finding something self-evident, or some kind of a proof about what proofs must be, then she wins the debate and the skeptic loses. Otherwise the skeptic wins. Why? Well, because then the questions will always have the upper hand, and that is what a skeptic wants.[1]

- *God.* Deities come up in dialectics mostly as first movers or final aims, and to have God is most often to have an intelligent self at the beginning or at the end of time, or both. But there are also dialectical arguments for God as the highest judge, that is as the top of a hierarchy of ethical authorities (for all

---

[1] Refuting the skeptic is a philosophical project. It is not scientific. A scientist normally takes some facts as givens and builds on these. She does not doubt everything she can. Similarly, mathematicians prove things but a proof of proofs would take one to philosophy (for example the philosophy of mathematics, or to the philosophy of logic, or to epistemology). The radical or extreme questions are not the scientists' but the philosophers'.

times), and also as something present everywhere in reality. Whatever the exact argument is, all dialectical theologies and religions are something reasoned. They do not invoke experiences of miracles, for example, or the authority of sacred texts or social elites. They are about *proving* the reality of God, by means of reasoned argument. All theologies and religions are not about proving or reasoning, but all dialectics are.[1]

There are also other dialectics. Some have attempted to view all of *history* dialectically, or all of *organic nature*, or *language*. In Chapter 4 we will see that Marx views *material production* dialectically.[2]

---

[1] I should note at this point that *all* reasoning is not dialectical, or at least everything that ordinarily get to be *called* reasoning by philosophers these days is not dialectical. Perhaps the most frequently studied kind of reasoning is deductive. Now, only some deductions are dialectical in this book's terms, namely those which deduce either *from* or *to* what is self-relational. One may try to analyze Plato's *Republic* or Descartes' *Meditations* in either way. (Of them only Plato is a self-aware dialectician, Descartes is not. Descartes does not think, or know, that he is doing dialectics. Instead, he thinks that he is doing something entirely new.)
Deductions by computers, mathematicians, lawyers, etc., are rarely foundational or dialectical. It is usual merely to assume certain rules as givens and to operate on their basis, not minding that the foundations are inexistent or unknown. For Plato and Descartes such customs are not rational enough. They would not call them reasoning. But it is rare to find anyone this strict these days. Today philosophers tend to act more like scientists, taking certain things for granted. For a recent discussion of foundationalism see BonJour.
[2] No one should think that this little book covers the *whole* history of dialectics. Here are some things I will devote less attention to than they deserve:
- *East Asian religions.* There is no doubt that these often precede Western sources. But studying them seriously would take me too far afield. I do not know enough about them yet to write about them properly. (I am a victim of Western biases in education! I was taught Plato but not Buddha.)
- *Aristotle.* Aristotle's philosophy is extremely rich but Aristotle's view of dialectics is too modest to be of great interest. Aristotle believes that he can reach grand conclusions in philosophy by doing empirical science, and this leads to all kinds of complications because *modern* science, as it has evolved, does not permit the big thinking that Aristotle likes (about God etc.). But the issues about science would require a different book. Aristotle cannot be confronted here.
- *Hegel.* Hegel gets little attention in this book because Hegel's dialectics are so dazzling as to easily overwhelm new readers. It is better to begin by acquiring clear tools for reasoning. Later one can try for what Hegel does, namely to understand great complexes in history and thought and to fit everything together.
I am sure that readers will have their own preferences about these sources and I will do my best to suggest further readings for everyone.

Does one really *need* dialectics? Are they important? Do they advance something or not?

One way to make these questions concrete is by asking whether we cannot all think for ourselves without special technical aids. Do we not all have our own thoughts, and should we not think exactly as we wish? *Die Gedanken sind frei*, rings an old German song that the persecuted have sung in prison: Thoughts are free.

There is indeed something to support this. Perhaps we cannot *move* as we wish or eat as we wish, but think? We can *wish* as we wish. We can *think* as we wish. Right? Is this not the unlimited terrain where we can fly as we like?

One can admit this quite liberally and still notice how studying thought does have some possible advantages, like these:

There are *stimulating problems*, which one may not have thought of. There are indeed very many problems in the general area of dialectics. Probably it is safe to say that no one has thought of them all. There is a lot in Hinduism, and a lot in Aristotle, but everything? No. Everything is nowhere. No matter how keen a mind one may take oneself to be, it is predictable that there is a great deal more waiting out there, in the dialectical literature. No one is quite cosmopolitan or awake, so everyone needs waking up. This is one reason to study dialectics.

There are *generative structures*. Sometimes anyone's thinking gets rather impotent, running too quickly to repetition or dead ends. Meanwhile there often are perfectly valid solutions which take one beyond the repetition. Individuals can find that they are capable of shaping ideas and habits they had never dreamed of before. For there are logical and grammatical tools which enhance our mental trajectories. One can become more original, and one can find what is more authentic and more one's own. A wealth of logics and grammars exist, and many can be used in dialectics. And again: no one has them all. Here is a second motive for learning about dialectics.

There are *victories of the understanding*. Many report feelings of pleasure on discovering analogies between different philosophies and theologies. There is a certain calm in coming to understand that humans everywhere face the same deep issues, apparently in every period and region. This provides one with a sense of belonging. It communicates a value of "humanism." This harmonious sentiment is often expressed in the Renaissance and in Romanticism. It is, arguably, one of the dialectician's unique entitlements.

In general, the point of dialectics is not to offend anyone but to open new doors. It is a world of possibilities.

I want to dwell on this third benefit of dialectics. Dialectics keep *returning*, over and over again in human history.

New human individuals are born and they ask the same questions, generation after generation. They do not ask only in Greek or German but in all languages. The topics are not specifically "Western" or "Eastern," or ancient or modern. In this way they are different from, say, fashions. Fashions are local, and each of them comes and goes, but dialectics keep coming back everywhere.[1]

This says something about their character. They are, as noted, something relational. They are not there in the details. They are, metaphorically,

- forests, not individual trees,
- melodies, not separate notes, or
- sentences, not words or letters.

They are patterns, not the individual particles that make up those patterns. Therefore, you can exchange the individuals or parts and nonetheless the same relations can come back.[2]

---

[1] This can prompt some readers to ask whether dialectics are like Jung's "Collective Unconscious." In some versions they are. Jung's archetypes do resemble Plato's Forms or Ideas, which are embedded in Plato's dialectics (see Chapter 2). Some, like Kant (Chapter 3) and Jaspers would say rather that what is innate to humans is a set of fundamental questions which do not have answers. For Plato and Jung we have guides, in the Forms or the archetypes, but for Kant and Jaspers we have none, because we are just born with questions — and no answers.

[2] A metaphysically curious side of dialectics is that you can often *exchange* the particles for others and still retain the patterns. That is, just as you can play the same melody on a flute as you can on a piano, or use smoke signals as well as Russian to count to ten, or run the same software on different kinds of computers, just so, in the same general way, you can also do dialectics in different symbols, using different media. Put differently, take away any material you like and the dialectics will remain there anyway. Let the world suddenly do without smoke signals — no problem, we will use pencils on paper instead. Take away paper and pencils — again no problem, we will use the Morse code now, etc. Why is this? Because dialectics are structural. It does not matter what the pattern is made of; it matters what the pattern is. You can draw a circle in the air with your finger or on paper with a pencil. You could use rocks to form a circle, like at Stonehenge. You can get the circle no matter what material you happen to have: a pencil, rocks, whatever.

This suggests that it would be absurd to say that dialectics are *material*, in the way that pencils and rocks are material. For clearly you do not need pencils or rocks at all to have circles. So, are dialectics spiritual? Well, they happen to be emotional, often, because their stakes get rather high. And perhaps no one has ever found a dialectic that was not in fact formed by a human mind in some kind of language. So perhaps dialectics are spiritual, if this is what "spiritual" means. But this book will not take things in that general direction. This book drives things

CHAPTER 1. ZENO

Tí tákhiston? Noûs. Dià pantòs gàr trékhei.
(Greek for: What is the fastest? The mind. It travels through everything.)

— Thales

Zeno lived in ancient Greece, at a time when traditional religions and social norms were quickly losing their authority. Competing schools of philosophy sought to fill the vacuum that opened. This was a period in which strong individualistic currents flowed. Many of the so-called "pre-Socratic" philosophers formulated viewpoints which remain incontestably deep and original to this day.[1] After Socrates, in contrast, philosophy acquired not only its own stable name but a more professional aura and a comparatively eclectic content. Then the era of the great originals was already past.

Zeno became famous for his paradoxes. Only some of these are safely credited to him (though some sources state that he had many more), and we will focus on three: the Achilles, the Arrow, and the Dichotomy. How they are solved is most easily learned from Aristotle. Plato's *Parmenides* gives the most likely explanation for *why* Zeno offered problems like these. Yet what we need to emphasize most, in this book on dialectical thought patterns, is actually Zeno's indirect *method*. For it is important to understand, at

---

towards ethics, that is, to questions about how it is best to live and think. Questions about what exists, spiritually or materially, are not the main ones here (Chapters 2 and 3 will explain why).
[1] On them see Snell, Jaeger (vol. 1), and Mourelatos.

this early stage in the book, why Zeno does not just teach us certain truths. Why does he begin with falsities and dead ends and questions that drive you mad? Why does he not just come out and tell us what he wants in a straight-forward way? There are reasons for this, as we will soon see.

1.1 The Achilles

Zeno uses several paradoxes to prove the impossibility of motion. The most famous is about Achilles and the turtle. The turtle and Achilles are in a running competition and at first the turtle is ahead of Achilles. But Achilles is faster. Now, Zeno argues that nonetheless Achilles can never reach the turtle! Why not? Because when the race begins, Achilles is at point a and the tortoise is further, at point b, but by the time Achilles reaches point b the tortoise is already at point c, and when Achilles reaches c the tortoise has already made it to d, etc. So though Achilles is faster than the turtle, he can never reach it.

If this is a valid problem, then it does not help to give Achilles more *time*, of course, because even if we give him an eternity the turtle will always have an advantage over Achilles, however slight that advantage may become eventually.

Zeno's paradox is disturbing because of course we feel that Achilles, being faster, *will* reach the turtle if only there is enough time. But this is just what Zeno intends. He wants to dumbfound us. His desired conclusion, that there is really no such thing as motion at all (a doctrine of his mentor Parmenides), is counter-intuitive. It is not common-sensical. So we *need* to be shocked somehow, or we can never wise up, Zeno would say.

1.2 The Arrow

The paradox of the flying Arrow is that if an arrow is said to fly, then at every particular *moment* when the arrow is flying it is nonetheless in a particular location and not in motion. So there is no moment at which the arrow flies or moves. But therefore there is no time at which the arrow flies.

1.3 The Dichotomy

Zeno's paradox of the Dichotomy is that before you travel a distance, from a to b, you must travel a half of that distance, and before you travel the half you must travel a fourth, and before the fourth an eighth, etc., and so on without limit. The conclusion is that you can never make it from a to b. You cannot possibly cover the distance, in any amount of time.

1.4 Aristotle's Solution

Many have attempted to identify faults in Zeno's arguments, from Aristotle to Bertrand Russell. Some of these attempts are highly technical. But luckily the solution need not be too complex. Already Aristotle seems to give us what we need to avoid Zeno's sharp arrows.

This is what Aristotle says (in his *Physics*, 233a21-31):

> Hence Zeno's argument makes a false assumption in asserting that it is impossible for a thing to pass over or severally to come in contact with infinite things in a finite time. For there are two senses in which length and time and generally anything continuous are called 'infinite': they are called so either in respect of divisibility or in respect of their extremities. So while a thing in a finite time cannot come in contact with things quantitatively infinite, it can come in contact with things infinite in respect of divisibility: for in this sense the time itself is also infinite: and so we find that the time occupied by the passage over the infinite is not a finite but an infinite time, and the contact with the infinites is made by means of moments not finite but infinite in number.

What does this mean? Aristotle says that Zeno is actually confused. Due to this, the answer Zeno wants to get at — namely Parmenides' grand theory of the oneness of everything (see 1.5 below) — is unneeded. The problems of Zeno are not really problems.

Why not? Here is how I propose to interpret Aristotle. Just because you *can* (at least in thought) divide your friend into infinitely many pieces it does not follow that you *need* to touch all the smallest parts separately to have touched her at all. Zeno mixes two very different things together: our *ability* to divide things into infinitely many pieces, typically in our reflections, and our *need* to go through all the pieces individually for the sake of motion or contact. Just because we *can* divide does not mean we *must*. Our thinking is unlike our moving. Zeno does not observe the difference between thinking and moving and hence ends up in difficulties manufactured by himself.

This may not be illuminating at first. Let us look at the same point from a different angle. If you move at the rate of a foot per second then in every half of a second you will move a half of a foot. In a millionth of a second you will move a millionth of a foot, and so on. Now, just because I can cut the foot and the second into smaller pieces, looking at 1 foot/second as well as 0.000001 foot/second, it does not mean that *you* need to slow down at any moment. The counting and slicing is one thing, but the moving is another thing. Zeno is confusing them with each other. It does not take you forever to cover the distance of a foot: it takes exactly a second. What may take forever is my thinking about the smallest fragments of the foot. I can go into the smaller pieces, but you do not have to.

Aristotle has just told us, in our terms of feet in seconds, that to move a foot in a second is a perfectly valid way, simultaneously, to move through every *tenth* of a foot in *tenths* of a second. The movement is just the same. There is no need for pausing or slowing down. The 1 foot/second motion covers all the parts that it contains. You do not need a different pace of movement for the smaller parts. (Aristotle's above passage says that even if a thing is infinitely divisible you can come into contact with that thing in a finite period of time. This is what we are now asserting in different words.[1])

But was that not quite clear yet either? Perhaps this is especially pertinent, intuitively: if you move consistently at the speed of a foot per second then you do not need to *take aim* many times per second to cover fragments of the foot. You do not need, for the sake of moving at a foot per second, to say to yourself, "OK, now I will cover the next hundredth of a foot," or, having said that, interrupt yourself with "Let me now first cover a millionth of a foot, to start with." You do not need to do this dividing to move. (If you did you would slow down.) Rather, you can take all the pieces in one gulp! An ordinary step in a second swallows up all the little millionths and hundredths of the foot at once. No one who steps around needs to set smaller aims or think of the microstructure of millionths. You get all the small segments for *free* if you cover only the big portions and focus on them. Your *rate* takes care of all the fragments.

All we have said so far, about Aristotle's solution, is that you do not need to cut things into small pieces or aims to *move* and cover distances. In this way Zeno is wrong.

Now let us briefly consider what happens if you *do* choose to cut things into pieces and set the smaller aims. We can give you a pace of performing, say, two divisions, into halves, per second. If you keep this rate up we can say how far you get in a minute, in an hour, etc. This is as easy to count. But *now* you would be slowing down to cover

---

[1] Aristotle also says, in the same passage above, that you cannot, in a finite amount of time, cover a distance between two extreme points, A and B, if the distance between A and B is infinite.

smaller and smaller units in Zeno's sense. Your rate of performing the divisions would not slow down; but the pieces you would cover would get smaller all the time. But this is not something you need to indulge in to exhibit motion or touch bodies or cover distances. And that makes the difference for solving Zeno's paradoxes.

Is there a need to relate this solution to Zeno's individual paradoxes? If there is, it can easily be done. Let us take the Achilles first. Let us say that Achilles runs at 5.5 feet/second and the turtle at 0.5 feet/second. If they are, say, 20 feet apart initially then in every second Achilles will get 5 feet closer to the turtle. The distance of 20 feet will be caught up in 4 seconds, period.

Next the Arrow. If the arrow flies at 10 feet a second then in half a second it will fly 5 feet. In an instant of time, that is a point which does not at all extend, how far does the arrow fly? 0 feet. But, as Aristotle would explain to Zeno, motion does not consist of extensionless instants or points. Zeno makes it seem that every larger whole is only a series of parts. That is just not correct. You *can* divide wholes into parts but it does not follow that that is *all* the wholes are. To illustrate, just because Chen is your friend this does not mean that every piece of Chen is also your friend. You do not need to locate your friendship in his hair or/and his feet or/and his tongue, etc. Again, a melody is not only the individual notes that make it up. It is also the harmonic *relation* between the notes. *Patterns* matter, not just the smallest parts. This is what Zeno overlooks. (Recall what the Introduction said about relations, or about forests versus trees, sentences versus words, etc.)

Finally, the Dichotomy. If you walk at the speed of 1 foot per second and the distance you mean to cover is, say, 600 feet wide then you will, of course, have made it across the distance in exactly 600 seconds, that is 10 minutes. Period.

What can we still say to give Zeno, or some modern Zenoist, a friendly impression of understanding his mistake? We cannot give him credit for doing *good physics*.[1] We can give him credit for *anticipating dialectics*. Now let us begin to do this.

1.5 Plato's Why

Why does Zeno present his paradoxes? He must have some point in saying these things, one thinks.

---

[1] An alternative I am ignoring is that Zeno's paradoxes have *mathematically* interesting implications. On that alternative see Russell, "Mathematics and the Metaphysicans". For more on Aristotle's response to Zeno see Bostock.

In Plato's *Parmenides* there is one answer to this. In this dialogue "Socrates" begins his conversation with Zeno as follows:

What is your meaning, Zeno? Do you maintain that if being is many, it must be both like and unlike, and that this is impossible, for neither can the like be unlike, nor the unlike like—is that your position?

Just so, said Zeno.

And if the unlike cannot be like, or the like unlike, then according to you, being could not be many; for this would involve an impossibility. In all that you say have you any other purpose except to disprove the being of the many? and is not each division of your treatise intended to furnish a separate proof of this, there being in all as many proofs of the not-being of the many as you have composed arguments? Is that your meaning, or have I misunderstood you?

No, said Zeno; you have correctly understood my general purpose.

I see, Parmenides, said Socrates, that Zeno would like to be not only one with you in friendship but your second self in his writings too; he puts what you say in another way, and would fain make believe that he is telling us something which is new. For you, in your poems, say The All is one, and of this you adduce excellent proofs; and he on the other hand says There is no many; and on behalf of this he offers overwhelming evidence. You affirm unity, he denies plurality. And so you deceive the world into believing that you are saying different things when really you are saying much the same. This is a strain of art beyond the reach of most of us.

Yes, Socrates, said Zeno. But although you are as keen as a Spartan hound in pursuing the track, you do not fully apprehend the true motive of the composition, which is not really such an artificial work as you imagine; for what you speak of was an accident; there was no pretence of a great purpose; nor any serious intention of deceiving the world. The truth is, that these writings of mine were meant to protect the arguments of Parmenides against those who make fun of him and seek to show the many ridiculous and contradictory results which they suppose to follow from the affirmation of the one. My answer is addressed to the partisans of the many, whose attack I return with interest by retorting upon them that their hypothesis of the being of many, if carried out, appears to be still more ridiculous than the hypothesis of the being of one. Zeal for my master led me to write the book in the days of my youth, but some one stole the copy; and therefore I had no choice whether it should be published or not; the motive, however, of writing, was not the ambition of an elder man, but the pugnacity of a young one. This you do not seem to see, Socrates; though in other respects, as I was saying, your notion is a very just one.[1]

From this we learn that Zeno did not intend to be cryptic. He meant to refute Parmenides' critics in a straight forward sense. He was a defender and follower of Parmenides.

What did Parmenides say? Here is an excerpt from his philosophical poetry:

> [...] for the same things can be thought of and can be. [B3]
> [...] for what exceeds is thought. [B16]
> One story, one road, now is left: that it is. And on this there are signs aplenty that, being, it is ungenerated and indestructible, whole, of one kind and unwavering, and complete. Nor was it ever, nor will it be, since now it is, all together, one, continuous. For what generation will you seek for it? How, whence, did it grow? That it came from what is not I shall not allow you to say or think — for it is not sayable or thinkable that it is not. [B8.1–8.9]
> Thus it must either altogether be or not be. [B8.11]
> How might what is then perish? [...] [B8.19]
> Nor is it divided, since it all alike is. [B8.22]
> Hence, it is all continuous; for what is approaches what is. [B8.25]

At lines B3 and B16 Parmenides affirmed something fundamental to many Greek philosophers, namely the power of thought. He holds, boldly, that thought is the measure of things. Conversely, he does not respect experience as an authority. In this way he is like Thales and others before him and Pythagoras and Plato later on. Many Greek philosophers valued speculation more than empirical experimentation. (Hence it is not surprising that ancient Greek reasoning and mathematics evolved much further than did Greek empirical science. The Greeks did not develop measuring instruments like the microscope or the telescope. They did not see their need.)

The next lines (i.e., 8.1 etc.) above portray Parmenides' conception of a uniform and changeless reality. This is the view that Zeno sought to endorse according to Plato's *Parmenides*.[2]

Now we have seen what Zeno seems to have been after. But what happened in real history is not what Zeno intended. Things got more complex. Zeno was soon viewed as an inspiration for rather indirect patterns of thought. Next let us look at those, because they will take us to the doorstep of dialectics.

---

[1] 127C–128E.
[2] On the *Parmenides* see Curd.

1.6 The Indirect Why

Zeno is a dialectician only in an incomplete sense. This is because, though he establishes contradictions, or at least apparent contradictions, he does not solve these. Consequently we have no positive self-relations in Zeno, and therefore he has no dialectics. It is as if he only asked a question and left it unanswered. A complete version of a dialectician would need to do both, ask *and* answer.[1] (This is something we already noted early in the Introduction.)

Why does Zeno not answer his questions? He does not say. We can surmise, if we want, that he wanted his hearers or readers to work out the answer themselves. (Alternatively it could be that his aim was actually to teach that there is no answer. This would make him a "skeptic." Several French scholars have argued that Zeno was in fact a skeptic, and not a Parmenidean, *contra* Plato.[2]) If this was his reason then he thought like many others in the dialectical tradition, from Heraclitus and Socrates to Marx. Many dialecticians have wanted to surprise their audience with novel problems and questions. This way they have been able to activate others. This is quite a different pedagogical strategy from direct lecturing or preaching. If you ask your students questions, you make them think. If you give them answers, or give the answers too soon, then you make them ready-made products of thought. You will then not guide them to the processes of thinking. And hence you will actually make them your own passive followers. They will then do less, and then they will learn to do less on their own.

A different motivation for Zeno's paradoxical manner of communication would not be pedagogical so much as logical. Many philosophers have thought that if you want to show that something is true, then the best thing for you to do is to assume that it is false and to deduce a contradiction from this. This is a secure path used by logicians to this day. This is not only a pedagogical strategy, unlike in the preceding paragraph. For it is one thing to do x because x makes your hearers think and it is another to do x to *prove* y. How may Zeno be attempting this? Well, he would then be saying: OK, let us assume

---

[1] As we saw, Plato says in his *Parmenides* that Zeno was a follower of Parmenides. If this is true then Zeno may *have* had an answer to his own questions, namely the answer of Parmenides. But when he communicates his paradoxes he leaves the answers out. This is why we can view him as a teacher who teaches by questioning and problematizing.

[2] See Tannery.

that there is motion. Then, by implication, there are these paradoxes. Therefore, there is no motion.

While it is possible to doubt that Zeno subscribed to the pedagogical motive it is rather safe to assume that he subscribed to this logical one. Why? Well, it makes his arguments so sensible. The logical motive makes Zeno seem like a brilliant theorist and strategist, even if his particular paradoxes happen to be invalid! For his merit would be to have discovered a way to prove conclusions logically. (His general pattern would be right even if his particular uses of it are wrong.)

Indirect communication flourishes in Zeno's time and after. I do not claim to know for certain that he influenced the others. But the others made their appearance either during his lifetime or after.

One of them is Heraclitus. He says things like this:

> Unapparent harmony is better than apparent. [B 54]
>
> [...] For some children who were killing lice deceived him by saying: 'What we saw and caught we leave behind, what we neither saw nor caught we take with us.' [B 56]
>
> We step and do not step into the same rivers, we are and we are not. [B 49a]
>
> The uncomprehending, when they hear, are like the deaf. To them applies the saying: though present they are absent. [B 34]
>
> Immortals are mortals, mortals immortals; living their death, dying their life. [B 62]
>
> War is the father of all, king of all: some it has shown as gods, some as men; some it has made slaves, some free. [B 53]
>
> The people should fight for the law as for the city wall. [B 44]
>
> Soul has a self-increasing account. [B 115]

The first of these fragments, B 54, lays out Heraclitus' communicative principle. This is that one should not expose one's thought too plainly. Why not? The second fragment, B 56, explains this. Being in harmony with the Heraclitean principle of indirect communication it is not direct or plain or obvious. What do you think it means? It seems to say that if you can identify something clearly then you can get rid of it. In other words, if something is blurry to you, like a living question or a persistent riddle, then you will *not* get rid of it. It will keep living in your mind because you will not have been able to identify it properly. You cannot destroy what you cannot locate. In other words, cryptic contents like Heraclitus' should have the advantage of permanence. They are difficult to get rid of, and they keep puzzling hearers.

Next, we have a fragment, B 49a, saying, most famously, that we do and do not step into the same rivers twice. Similarly, the uncomprehending are present and absent at once, immortals die, mortals do not, and everything is at war (that is: in conflict). But this seems to be the permanent truth in Heraclitus' world, and apparently the thinker who thinks it raises herself or himself to a kind stability and position of oversight. I do not claim to know what Heraclitus means exactly, but he seems to say that the eternal law of things which one can ultimately discover consists of "war." Knowing that war is eternal would be a kind of peace.

Heraclitus' manner of indirect instruction is a little different from Zeno's, of course. (Zeno's dialectic is Elean, but Heraclitus' is Ionian, and the Elean Greeks philosophized differently from the Ionians.) Following Fränkel I will take the following pattern to be paradigmatic in Heraclitus' philosophy:

> Man is called a baby by god, even as a child by a man. [B 79]
>
> The most beautiful ape is ugly compared to man. [B 82]
>
> The wisest man is an ape compared to god. [B 83]

Here the central point of comparing an ape and a man and a god seems to be to say something about an unknown thing (god) by speaking of familiar things (apes, men). So it is as if Heraclitus were offering his readers a riddle, in effect saying "What stands to a man as a man stands to an ape?" In answering the riddle one would add substance behind the mysteriously empty word "god." That is, one would explain god by reference to the difference between the man and the ape. The same thing happens, of course, if we insert "baby" for "ape."[1]

Notice that at least sometimes Heraclitus' riddles can be solved in more than one way. For instance, if god stands to man like a man stands to a baby then the information that is being communicated about god can be that he (or she) is especially wise, tall, hairy, etc. (There is leeway unless one mentions such a thing as wisdom or beauty, as in B 82 and B 83.) The fragments are often only suggestive, in this way. They could be more than that, and they would have more singular solutions (instead of having many alternative solutions), if they contained more terms. Compare:

(a) ape: man: god.
(b) catRmouseRcheese.
(c) 1,2,4, ...
(d) 1,2,4,7,...
(e) 1,2,4,8,...
(f) "Juliet is the sun" (said by Romeo in Shakespeare's *Romeo and Juliet*).
(g) grandmotherRmotherRdaughter.

---

[1] This view of Heraclitus is derived from Fränkel.

(a) and (b) are ambiguous in a similar sense because they suggest several relations. R in (b) can stand for seeks, eats, is bigger than, is more of a pet than, etc. This is because each of these values for R makes (b) intelligible. In this way (a) and (b) are like (c), because (c), too, is ambiguous, namely between (d) and (e). (c) can be interpreted in either way, (d) or (e). (c) does not determine the choice between (d) and (e). This is a rather general fact about Heraclitus. He only *begins* certain series, or *sketches* problems. He does not go all the way to sharp paradoxes like Zeno. He leaves more of the intellectual labor to us. One may think that this is a nice thing of him to do, because it is more liberal. But it is also more risky, because if one communicates loosely then one does not compel anyone to take one's message seriously. Loose idioms make matters more voluntary. It appears that Heraclitus does not notice this implication of this method.

(f) is even looser than Heraclitus' loosest lines. (f) is ambiguous in the way that metaphors in literary works often are, and ambiguity is perhaps instanced with special clarity precisely by metaphors. Romeo may mean that Juliet is bright, warm, central to life, reliable, etc.; but he probably does not mean that she is yellow, round, or gaseous. Nonetheless what Romeo actually *says*, namely that Juliet is the sun, implies warmth or brightness just as much as it implies roundness or yellowness. Shakespeare, like Heraclitus, depends heavily on the goodwill of his readers. The reader must choose the sensible interpretations or the text is only silly.

Next recall that the ambiguity of (c) was avoided by adding terms, as in (d) or (e). Now, adding terms to a series is possible also by squeezing them in *between* prior terms, not only to the end of the series. Between (a)'s ape and man we could have a Neanderthal and between man and god we could insert some kind of a superman (or *Übermensch*, as in Nietzsche). This would also be a way to supply our expressions with determinacy if rhe superman has an independent reality that is familiar to us. But now we can understand something rather important about Zeno. For typically Zeno squeezes shorter distances and time-slices between longer ones. (If one has aRb then Zeno tries to squeeze more in between, making aRa'Rb, and then from there he wants to force you to aRa'Ra''Rb, etc. He will not let you get directly from a to b via R.) That is the formal trick he plays, over and over, to formulate his paradoxes.

However, I also want to bring up (g); (g) illustrates the fact that three terms can suffice to communicate a determinate relation, that is, a relation that is not ambiguous at all. For what may be followed by this relation? Only a further daughter. And what may be preceded by it? Only a great-grandmother. There are no choices. There is no leeway. Hence it would not be true to say that disambiguation must always proceed by adding more terms than three. Adding more terms helps sometimes but questions about logical determination are not always that simple.

I should mention that the formal patterns of communication we have been discussing in this chapter are far from being the only ones. We have focused on the patterns that matter most to dialectics at their simplest. The pre-Socratics foreshadow dialectics, and that is why we looked into them.

What other formal patterns are there? We should look at a few that will come up below. For one thing, one can use pairs:

(h) a:b::c:d, i.e.,

(i) a stands to b just like c stands to d, e.g.,

(j) 1:2::3:6, or

(k) Lisa is to the rest of the school what a dolphin is to all animals.

What is the relation in (k)? E.g., is more clever than, or is more playful than. How about in (j)? Times two makes. But notice that (j) is not the same as (l):

(l) 1:2::2:4.

In (l) we have a pair of pairs in which the same pattern repeats higher up and lower down. For not only are the pairs (1,2) and (2,4) drawn from the relation times two makes but the pair of pairs, ((1,2),(2,4)) obeys the same relation. This kind of a pair of pairs we will meet with pairs in Plato's *Phaedo* below. But its use will not lead to any major deviation from the more standard dialectical structures.

This suffices about Zeno and Heraclitus. Both are precursors to Socrates and now we can turn to him.[1]

---

[1] A further influence on Socrates' dialectic was that of the "sophists." They taught Greek youths for money, and their aim was to educate public speakers for the democratic *polis* of Athens. The association was that the ability to speak well in pubic amounted to an exercise of social power.
The reason why I do not elaborate on the sophists is that they teach us so little about dialectics. They are sources of diverse logical fallacies and rhetorical tropes, but these are not elements in serious dialectics. In other words, dialectic should not be *demeaned* by comparing it to rhetoric. (Who demeans dialectic like that? Aristotle, in his *Rhetoric*. Aristotle tends to ignore all the more serious aspects of dialectics.)

Further Reading

Jonathan Barnes: *The Pre-Socratic Philosophers.* This is a very accessible introduction. It is the source of some of my translations in this chapter.

Alexander Mourelatos, editor: *The Pre-Socratics.* Here is a collection of great in-depth scholarship on the pre-Socratics.

Bruno Snell: *The Discovery of the Mind.* This classic makes a consistent argument of its own and covers a lot of ground in little space.

(See the Bibliography at the end of this book for detailed information on these and other titles.)

Chapter 2. Socrates

Ho de anexetastos bios ou biôtos anthrôpôi.
(Greek for: The unexamined life is not worth living for a human being.)
— Socrates

Socrates' revolution in dialectics is ethical. For him it is not movement that is paradoxical, as it was for Zeno in the previous chapter, but thought, value, or action. In our ordinary lives we end up in contradictions when we set aims and use standards, not when we try to catch a turtle or walk across a plain. This makes Socrates' dialectic less optional to us than Zeno's. For one may choose to avoid Zeno's issues altogether, and brush him aside. One may lack interest in thoughts about chasing a turtle or about walking across a plain. But this same avoidance is not possible with Socrates, because Socrates' burning desire is to find out how to live one's life! He wants to identify plans and standards for actions. One cannot easily evade Socrates' questions and still be a living individual, who considers what to do and why. One can avoid questions about turtle-chasing, but one cannot avoid questions about life (except by dying, of course).

Socrates' message is not only paradoxical. He does not present us only with difficulties, and in this way, too, he differs from Zeno. Socrates' main concern is to communicate that we should live differently. We should *change*, becoming better. His dialectic is about what we should or must do, not only about what we must not. He tells us, or perhaps rather *shows* us, how to live in a way that avoids the big puzzles. But this difference between Zeno and Socrates should not be exaggerated, for we will presently see that also Socrates does set traps, and as a trap-setting philosopher he is an indirect teacher in Zeno's older tradition.

Socrates' indirect method is in important respects like Zeno's. Socrates asks questions of others and when he gets their answers he shows their contradictions. In this way he shows that his interlocutors are wrong by their *own* lights. His cleverness consists precisely in this. So there is the impression once more, as with Zeno, that teaching and communication must be oriented to problems. One should not present others with ready-made answers, preach to them, or only make them memorize things. One needs to activate them. *They* should figure things out. The ambition can even be to liberate them. On the analysis I will now offer of Socrates' dialectic its aim is to liberate thought. That is what it is fundamentally about all the time.

Socrates's dialectics have come down to us through Plato. Socrates only spoke and never wrote. In his earlier dialogues Plato seeks to report what Socrates said but later he attempts to extend Socrates' project. The more mature Plato wants to use dialectics to show that we have innate knowledge, that our souls or psyches are immortal, that a utopian society needs constructing, and that God exists. We need to be careful in assessing whether these results follow from Socrates' dialectic, and Plato seems to hold that they do.[1]

2.1 Self-Criticism

Socrates is the archetypal questioner. He is a kind of living question-mark. In Plato's *Apology* the story of his life is presented as follows.

First a religious oracle tells him that he is the wisest of all.

Second, he does not see, on his own, what the oracle can mean. So though Socrates is the wisest Socrates does not know *what* he knows, or how he is wise. He does not even know what knowledge or wisdom is. So he puzzled. What can the oracle mean?

Third, Socrates goes out to ask other people in Athens what wisdom is. But no matter whom he goes to he finds only vain self-confidence, never self-knowledge. For so many individuals *say* they know things but when they are supposed to *show* their knowledge, by supplying

---

[1] Plato's dialogues are commonly divided into three groups: early, middle, and late. The early dialogues are usually said to be true about the historically real Socrates. In the middle and late dialogues a fictional character by the name of "Socrates" appears as Plato's mouthpiece. (See Fine vol. 1 p. 1.) I will refer only to the early dialogues' Socrates' as Socrates.
(A further, "transitional" stage in Plato's career will also be distinguished later.)

proof, one finds that they do not really know. They only think they know. More exactly, each individual thinks that what he or she is used to doing is correct. The cobbler associates knowledge or skill with cobbling; the public speaker identifies it with an ability to explain; the mathematician believes that what is essential is counting; etc. The point is that if one has only a hammer one sees only nails, as the saying goes. Each individual exaggerates the importance of her own specialty, and each of them is therefore wrong!

Fourth, Socrates begins to suspect that he is wise in knowing that he does *not* know. For he seems to be the only one around who lacks epistemic self-reliance. He is the only one who asks, while everyone else is just answering. Everyone else is preaching so much that they cannot even hear each other. Only Socrates listens. Herein is his wisdom.

Here are some excerpts from the *Apology,* conveying the situation in Socrates' own words:

> When I left him, I reasoned thus with myself: I am wiser than this man, for neither of us appears to know anything great and good; but he fancies he knows something, although he knows nothing; whereas I, as I do not know anything, so I do not fancy I do.[1]

> O Athenians! I honor and love you; but I shall obey God rather than you; and so long as I breathe and am able, I shall not cease studying philosophy, and exhorting you and warning any one of you I may happen to meet, saying, as I have been accustomed to do: 'O best of men! seeing you are an Athenian, of a city the most powerful and most renowned for wisdom and strength, are you not ashamed of being careful for riches, how you may acquire them in greatest abundance, and for glory, and honor, but care not nor take any thought for wisdom and truth, and for your soul, how it may be made most perfect?'[2]

> And if any one of you should question my assertion, and affirm that he does care for these things, I shall not at once let him go, nor depart, but I shall question him, sift and prove him. And if he should appear to me not to possess virtue, but to pretend that he does, I shall reproach him for that he sets the least value on things of the greatest worth, but the highest on things that are worthless.[3]

> Thus I shall act to all whom I meet, both young and old, stranger and citizen [...].[4]

> For, if you should put me to death, you will not easily find such another, though it may be ridiculous to say so, altogether attached by

---

[1] 21D.
[2] 29D–E.
[3] 29E–30A.
[4] 30A.

the deity to this city as to a powerful and generous horse, somewhat sluggish from his size, and requiring to be roused by a gad-fly; so the deity appears to have united me, being such a person as I am, to the city, that I may rouse you, and persuade and reprove every one of you, nor ever cease besetting you throughout the whole day. Such another man, O Athenians! will not easily be found [...].[1]

But neither did I then think that I ought, for the sake of avoiding danger, to do any thing unworthy of a freeman, nor do I now repent of having so defended myself; but I should much rather choose to die, having so defended myself, than to live in that way. For neither in a trial nor in battle is it right that I or anyone else should employ every possible means whereby he may avoid death; for in battle it is frequently evident that a man might escape death by laying down his arms, and throwing himself on the mercy of his pursuers. And there are many other devices in every danger, by which to avoid death, if a man dares to do and say every thing. But this is not difficult, O Athenians! to escape death; but it is much more difficult to avoid depravity, for it runs swifter than death.[2]

Only the examined life is worth living, Socrates says. One should focus on living well, not long, so it is quality and not quantity that matters. Social esteem and death are small stuff compared to questions of principle. One needs to have great relations to great things and small relations to small things, but Socrates' Athenians have this upside down. Socrates is the gadfly, stinging Athens awake with his criticisms. He will never stop doing this, as long as he lives.

But what happens, it turns out soon after Socrates has held a speech to the public in which he says all this, is that Athens prefers to go on sleeping. Socrates is condemned to death. The democratic majority of Athens sentences him to this penalty. (In the Athenian direct democracy, the citizens acted as the jury and the judge, by simple majority voting.) He is charged with corrupting the young, denying gods, inventing gods, saying of inexistent things that they exist, and saying that existent things do not exist. In short, if Socrates thinks that Athens has things backwards, the Athenians throw this same allegation right back at him. They are at loggerheads.

In the short term, Athens wins. Socrates is silenced. But later in history Socrates' self-critical trait has been very widely celebrated and copied. Socrates is the hero not only of Plato, whom we will come to soon. He is admired and copied also by Hellenic Stoics, skeptics, and cynics, and later by the Renaissance humanist Erasmus of Rotterdam,

---

[1] 30E–31A.
[2] 38E–39A.

Romantics and existentialists like Johann Georg Hamann and Søren Kierkegaard, and, in our own age, by the anti-totalitarian philosophers Karl Popper and Hannah Arendt, who write about totalitarianism soon after the Second World War. It is notable that in an essential sense the image of Socrates does not change throughout this history of reception, because thinkers are consistent in valuing his humility, no matter what backgrounds they come from. The Buddha and Jesus have been admired and followed for similar reasons. On a deep level Socrates belongs with them, even if he is not religious in trusting that there is a here-after. He lacks that kind of trust, but on the other hand he is logically sharp and critical in a way that the more easily trusting personalities are not. His humility is different, but arguably it is equally significant.

How could an individual like Socrates emerge? What formed him? The Athens of Socrates' time is full of all kinds of preachers and esoteric religions. There are religious festivals for different sects nearly every second day. The religions are colorful, emotional, often wildly physical and sometimes violent. Mysteries and sensations are everywhere. It is, on a modern comparison, like living in a world full of low-quality newspapers which report sensational stories about celebrities and aliens from outer space. In other words, the liberal Athenian social climate is filling up with nonsense. That is when Socrates arrives on the scene.

When Socrates makes his entry he is exotic in a kind of reversed sense. For among the immodest he is the only one who is modest. Among the loud he alone is quiet. Everyone claims to have answers, but only Socrates is full of questions. Everyone knows except Socrates.

This contrast is not utterly unlike that between Jesus and the early Christians in the Roman culture of the early centuries A.D. The Romans indulge in extreme barbarism, eating and drinking until they vomit, roaring with applause in the Coliseum shows where beasts slaughter and mate with humans and each other. Rome becomes so decadent that the only sensation that is impressive anymore is Christianity. The only miracles left are modesty, mercy, and honesty.[1]

---

[1] Nietzsche says that Socrates causes a sweeping change in the cultural history of ancient Greece. Before Socrates the Greeks admire the heroism of the Homeric Achilles, but after Socrates the main object of fascination becomes the myth of the dying Socrates (*Birth of Tragedy*, § 15). Nietzsche is keenly aware that Socrates has certain deep similarities with Jesus. Of course, it is the death of *Christ* that is central to Christians, but this is not an entirely different matter. Many Christian associations regarding death and spirituality go back to Socrates and Plato (see Plato's *Phaedo* in particular; meanwhile Plato's *Timaeus* is a main source of Christian creationism).

2.2 The Criticism of Others

Even in the *Apology* Socrates' critical energies are often directed outward, but that work contains little of the cross-questioning that Socrates typically conducts. Here is how he normally teaches his philosophy to others:

First he asks questions of an individual who tries to answer them.

Second, he gets the individual to bring her values to a focal point. This is when the individual produces a definition of a value that is central to her life, such as courage, justice, wisdom, pleasure, piety, etc.

Third, Socrates checks whether the individual can generalize the same value-definition for all circumstances, or else abstract it from all possible contexts and ascribe it value in isolation; and this is when Socrates finds that the individual cannot do these things. What the individual defines as courageous is not in fact courageous. Hence contradictions or paradoxes ensue.

Fourth, Socrates concludes that the individual has refuted herself. And for this reason she should also learn to say, like Socrates, *I do not know. You tell me.* That is: *Finally now I am pure and wise when I have shed my earlier illusions and self-importance!* The interlocutors may even be taught to go as far as this: *Now I need to go question others, now I need to go out and be a new Socrates!*

In essence, Socratic instruction is all about being refuted. Before one is refuted in one's beliefs it is difficult for one to draw limits to one's knowledge, but after the refutation there is fresh air again and one's mind is open. One is rejuvenated and made more pleasant to deal with than one was in one's earlier state of pride.

All this is easier to understand from examples.

There are many examples of this same procedure in the early Platonic dialogues. I propose that we move directly to the most troubling ones. Two figures are especially remote from Socrates' ethical mindset: Callicles and Thrasymachus. They preach power politics and greed with particular vehemence. Here is Callicles from Plato's *Gorgias:*

> CALLICLES: What innocence! you mean those fools,—the temperate?
>
> SOCRATES: Certainly:—anyone may know that to be my meaning.

For a different comparison between Socrates and Christ see Kierkegaard. Kierkegaard, being a Christian, views Socrates as a less complete version of Christ. Nietzsche is an atheist whose view of Christ is often very negative. Nietzsche's relationship to Socrates oscillates between love and hate.

CALLICLES: Quite so, Socrates; and they are really fools, for how can a man be happy who is the servant of anything? On the contrary, I plainly assert, that he who would truly live ought to allow his desires to wax to the uttermost, and not to chastise them; but when they have grown to their greatest he should have courage and intelligence to minister to them and to satisfy all his longings. And this I affirm to be natural justice and nobility. To this however the many cannot attain; and they blame the strong man because they are ashamed of their own weakness, which they desire to conceal, and hence they say that intemperance is base. As I have remarked already, they enslave the nobler natures, and being unable to satisfy their pleasures, they praise temperance and justice out of their own cowardice. For if a man had been originally the son of a king, or had a nature capable of acquiring an empire or a tyranny or sovereignty, what could be more truly base or evil than temperance—to a man like him, I say, who might freely be enjoying every good, and has no one to stand in his way, and yet has admitted custom and reason and the opinion of other men to be lords over him?—must not he be in a miserable plight whom the reputation of justice and temperance hinders from giving more to his friends than to his enemies, even though he be a ruler in his city? Nay, Socrates, for you profess to be a votary of the truth, and the truth is this:—that luxury and intemperance and license, if they be provided with means, are virtue and happiness—all the rest is a mere bauble, agreements contrary to nature, foolish talk of men, nothing worth.

SOCRATES: There is a noble freedom, Callicles, in your way of approaching the argument; for what you say is what the rest of the world think, but do not like to say.[1]

If you can rob others and get away with it, do it! That is what Callicles is saying. Never mind any social codes, because they are only artificial fabrications of the weak to dominate the strong.

Thrasymachus' angle is not very different in the first book of the *Republic*. There Socrates narrates:

Several times in the course of the discussion Thrasymachus had made an attempt to get the argument into his own hands, and had been put down by the rest of the company, who wanted to hear the end. But when Polemarchus and I had done speaking and there was a pause, he could no longer hold his peace; and, gathering himself up, he came at us like a wild beast, seeking to devour us. We were quite panic-stricken at the sight of him.

He roared out to the whole company: What folly, Socrates, has taken possession of you all? And why, sillybillies, do you knock under

---

[1] 491E–492D.

to one another? I say that if you want really to know what justice is, you should not only ask but answer, and you should not seek honour to yourself from the refutation of an opponent, but have your own answer; for there is many a one who can ask and cannot answer. And now I will not have you say that justice is duty or advantage or profit or gain or interest, for this sort of nonsense will not do for me; I must have clearness and accuracy.

I was panic-stricken at his words, and could not look at him without trembling. Indeed I believe that if I had not fixed my eye upon him, I should have been struck dumb: but when I saw his fury rising, I looked at him first, and was therefore able to reply to him.

Thrasymachus, I said, with a quiver, don't be hard upon us. Polemarchus and I may have been guilty of a little mistake in the argument, but I can assure you that the error was not intentional. If we were seeking for a piece of gold, you would not imagine that we were "knocking under to one another," and so losing our chance of finding it. And why, when we are seeking for justice, a thing more precious than many pieces of gold, do you say that we are weakly yielding to one another and not doing our utmost to get at the truth? Nay, my good friend, we are most willing and anxious to do so, but the fact is that we cannot. And if so, you people who know all things should pity us and not be angry with us.

How characteristic of Socrates! he replied, with a bitter laugh;— that's your ironical style! Did I not foresee—have I not already told you, that whatever he was asked he would refuse to answer, and try irony or any other shuffle, in order that he might avoid answering?[1] [...] Listen, then, he said; I proclaim that justice is nothing else than the interest of the stronger. And now why do you not praise me? But of course you won't.

Let me first understand you, I replied. Justice, as you say, is the interest of the stronger. What, Thrasymachus, is the meaning of this? You cannot mean to say that because Polydamas, the pancratiast, is stronger than we are, and finds the eating of beef conducive to his bodily strength, that to eat beef is therefore equally for our good who are weaker than he is, and right and just for us?

That's abominable of you, Socrates; you take the words in the sense which is most damaging to the argument.

Not at all, my good sir, I said; I am trying to understand them; and I wish that you would be a little clearer.

Well, he said, have you never heard that forms of government differ; there are tyrannies, and there are democracies, and there are aristocracies?

---

[1] 336B–337A.

Yes, I know.

And the government is the ruling power in each state?

Certainly.

And the different forms of government make laws democratical, aristocratical, tyrannical, with a view to their several interests; and these laws, which are made by them for their own interests, are the justice which they deliver to their subjects, and him who transgresses them they punish as a breaker of the law, and unjust. And that is what I mean when I say that in all states there is the same principle of justice, which is the interest of the government; and as the government must be supposed to have power, the only reasonable conclusion is, that everywhere there is one principle of justice, which is the interest of the stronger.[1]

Thrasymachus is aware of Socrates' clever strategies of argument and views them only as a childish game. In the real world, he says, only might counts. Whoever happens to be in power makes the rules, and that is all that really ever speaks for the rules.

How is the view of Callicles and Thrasymachus to be understood or evaluated? From Socrates' angle their view is not particularly dangerous in content. For, like Thomas Hobbes and Friedrich Nietzsche in modern times, they theorize about justice on a factual basis. They generalize about the normal course of events in different societies. This is to shoot past Socrates' target issue because Socrates' questions always concern values and not facts. That is, Socrates is always interested in what *should* exist, or in what *must* be done, and never in what *already* exists or what is *usually* done.

Hence, the difficulty with Callicles and Thrasymachus is not a rational difficulty. There is little danger that what they say might turn out to be right. For they have merely misunderstood Socrates' questions. But the real difficulty is in making *them* see this. For Callicles and Thrasymachus do not subscribe to the *ethos* of mutual questioning. Mutual questioning does not exhibit the kind of power that they celebrate. On the contrary, for them mutual questioning is a value of the weak. Socrates engages in mutual questioning because he is afraid of direct physical contests of force, they imply. Socrates is indirect and cunning precisely because he is weak, they hold. Hence, the very *axioms* of Callicles and Thrasymachus are opposed to Socrates. They do not scorn his conclusions only. They scorn his very *method*. How, then, can Socrates try to convert them? Will every question not be begged on

---

[1] 338C–339A.

both sides? Is Socrates not simply at loggerheads with someone once again?

This is when we notice how cunning Socrates' method actually is. For he gets Thrasymachus and Callicles to refute *themselves*. He gets them to give an answer and then also to contradict that same answer. Therefore, it is not by *Socrates'* standards that they fail, but by their own! Hence, it is as if Socrates only showed them a mirror. It is not his fault what is seen in the mirror when they look into it. If Socrates succeeds in making this plain to them then he was won the game. Then the moral lesson will have been drawn, even if Callicles and Thrasymachus do not in fact change their ways entirely after their short contacts with Socrates. For then the rational moral is there, and every open-minded reader will perceive it.

How *would* Socrates' practice change these men, *if* it did? What would be exchanged for what in their lives? Manipulative efforts would be exchanged for efforts to learn from others. That is the moral conversion implicit in Socrates' practice. This is the kind of morality he represents by acting as he does. This is also the kind of morality that others should be led to adopt through contacts with him. If you will, he is the extreme questioner, the archetype; and Callicles and Thrasymachus and everyone else are to copy him, if they cannot beat him at his game.

But how, exactly, does Socrates get Thrasymachus and Callicles to contradict themselves? This is something we have not yet explained, and it demands that we inspect Socrates' characteristic paradoxes.

2.3 Paradoxes

There are many paradoxes in Socrates but I will here head straight for the main one.[1] We can call it the *Paradox of Ends*.

---

[1] Paradoxes in Socrates (and Plato) really come in two groups. There are paradoxes which consist of *logical self-contradictions*, and these I will deal with in the main text. To this group belong what I call the Paradox of Ends and also what is commonly labled the Paradox of Inquiry (see 2.7 below). But then there are also paradoxes which consist merely of *unusual views*. They are against (Greek: *para*) commonly held views (Greek: *doxa*). Here are some notes about this latter goup of paradoxes, which I will not be coming back to later.
One Socratic paradox in this vein is that virtue is the same as knowledge. This is to say that if you know what to do, then automatically you will do it. Conversely, if you do not do it, that shows that you do not know that you should. So there is no weakness of the will for Socrates, unlike for instance for Aristotle. In Aristotle's view one must train the emotions and get used to all kinds of practical habits if one is to advance in one's actions. Intellectual realizations are not

In the *Gorgias* it is formulated in this way:

SOCRATES: Well, I will tell you another image, which comes out of the same school:—Let me request you to consider how far you would accept this as an account of the two lives of the temperate and intemperate in a figure:—There are two men, both of whom have a number of casks; the one man has his casks sound and full, one of wine, another of honey, and a third of milk, besides others filled with other liquids, and the streams which fill them are few and scanty, and he can only obtain them with a great deal of toil and difficulty; but when his casks are once filled he has no need to feed them anymore, and has no further trouble with them or care about them. The other, in like manner, can procure streams, though not without difficulty; but his vessels are leaky and unsound, and night and day he is compelled to be filling them, and if he pauses for a moment, he is in an agony of pain. Such are their respective lives:—And now would you say that the life of the intemperate is happier than that of the temperate? Do I not convince you that the opposite is the truth?

CALLICLES: You do not convince me, Socrates, for the one who has filled himself has no longer any pleasure left; and this, as I was just now saying, is the life of a stone: he has neither joy nor sorrow after he is once filled; but the pleasure depends on the superabundance of the influx.

SOCRATES: But the more you pour in, the greater the waste; and the holes must be large for the liquid to escape.

CALLICLES: Certainly.

---

enough for behavioral development, Aristotle says. But Socrates is an "intellectualist," thinking that we are ruled by our thoughts. Changes in thoughts suffice for changing lives.

A second Socratic paradox of this looser kind is that only one thing is virtuous. This contrasts with the widely held view that there are many worthwhile ways to live, for instance one for women and another for men, or one in Ethiopia and one to go by when in Egypt. For Socrates there is only one standard for everyone and everywhere, for rich or poor, in the West and the East. This can sound narrow-minded but it is also egalitarian, in a way that, for example, Aristotle's philosophy is not. If you use a different standard for someone, you are putting that person lower or higher. That is what it normally means. (Moreover, to work with a single highest standard is nicely consistent and rational, and working with two standards easily leads to inconsistency.)

A third paradox in Socrates is that the unjust suffer more than their victims. The point of this one is that your soul or character suffers if you do not act on idealistic enough a standard. You demean yourself if you start stealing and bickering, for example. But harming others requires that you go low in that way, Socrates says.

On Socrates' paradoxes, see Prior. On Aristotle's views in ethics, see his *Nicomachean Ethics*.

SOCRATES: The life which you are now depicting is not that of a dead man, or of a stone, but of a cormorant; you mean that he is to be hungering and eating?

CALLICLES: Yes.

SOCRATES: And he is to be thirsting and drinking?

CALLICLES: Yes, that is what I mean; he is to have all his desires about him, and to be able to live happily in the gratification of them.[1]

The lifestyle of Callicles is one of strong desires and much waste. You are to need much and to use much. Once you have had your fill you are to expose yourself to needs and cravings again. You seek thirst so that you may enjoy drink, but right after drinking you seek thirst again. This lifestyle is "intemperate" because it is not about controlling your appetites. It is rather about being controlled *by* one's appetites. Socrates is saying that this way of life is problematic somehow. But how?

The problem Socrates is hinting at in the preceding passage is brought out more explicitly in the *Lysis*. As usual Socrates instructs by questioning:

The sick man, as I was just now saying, is the friend of the physician—is he not?

Yes.

And he is the friend of the physician because of disease, and for the sake of health?

Yes.

And disease is an evil?

Certainly.

And what of health? I said. Is that good or evil, or neither?

Good, he replied.

And we were saying, I believe, that the body being neither good nor evil, because of disease, that is to say because of evil, is the friend of medicine, and medicine is a good: and medicine has entered into this friendship for the sake of health, and health is a good.

True.

And is health a friend, or not a friend?

A friend.

And disease is an enemy?

Yes.

---

[1] 493D–494C.

Then that which is neither good nor evil is the friend of the good because of the evil and hateful, and for the sake of the good and the friend?

Clearly.

Then the friend is a friend for the sake of the friend, and because of the enemy?

That is to be inferred.

Then at this point, my boys, let us take heed, and be on our guard against deceptions. I will not again repeat that the friend is the friend of the friend, and the like of the like, which has been declared by us to be an impossibility; but, in order that this new statement may not delude us, let us attentively examine another point, which I will proceed to explain: Medicine, as we were saying, is a friend, or dear to us for the sake of health?

Yes.

And health is also dear?

Certainly.

And if dear, then dear for the sake of something?

Yes.

And surely this object must also be dear, as is implied in our previous admissions?

Yes.

And that something dear involves something else dear?

Yes.

But then, proceeding in this way, shall we not arrive at some first principle of friendship or dearness which is not capable of being referred to any other, for the sake of which, as we maintain, all other things are dear, and, having there arrived, we shall stop?

True.

My fear is that all those other things, which, as we say, are dear for the sake of another, are illusions and deceptions only, but where that first principle is, there is the true ideal of friendship. Let me put the matter thus: Suppose the case of a great treasure (this may be a son, who is more precious to his father than all his other treasures); would not the father, who values his son above all things, value other things also for the sake of his son? I mean, for instance, if he knew that his son had drunk hemlock, and the father thought that wine would save him, he would value the wine?

He would.

And also the vessel which contains the wine?

Certainly.

But does he therefore value the three measures of wine, or the earthen vessel which contains them, equally with his son? Is not this rather the true state of the case? All his anxiety has regard not to the means which are provided for the sake of an object, but to the object for the sake of which they are provided. And although we may often say that gold and silver are highly valued by us, that is not the truth; for there is a further object, whatever it may be, which we value most of all, and for the sake of which gold and all our other possessions are acquired by us. Am I not right?

Yes, certainly.

And may not the same be said of the friend? That which is only dear to us for the sake of something else is improperly said to be dear, but the truly dear is that in which all these so-called dear friendships terminate.

That, he said, appears to be true.

And the truly dear or ultimate principle of friendship is not for the sake of any other or further dear.

True.[1]

This is a familiar pattern. In the Introduction we labeled it "R3." Medicine is dear for the sake of health, and health may be dear for the sake of something else. Socrates is looking for a termination for this series. If we begin from aR3bR3c... then the termination is ...zR3z or ...zR3R3. Without any technical symbols the question is simply: What will be dear for its own sake? This is what Socrates is asking. Medicine, for example, is not that, because it is dear only for the sake of health. Consequently it is not really or properly dear at all, as such. It is based on something else. Its dearness is only parasitic, or relative. It is not absolute or self-sufficient. So what has dearness as such? Where can one go if one wants to find satisfaction instead of only running around like this from milestone to meaningless milestone?

The scenario Socrates is describing is like one from a "rat race," that is a race that cannot be won. For whenever you get a hold of your aim it slips away again. Another image is of a carrot held with a stick in front of a donkey. The donkey walks forward to get towards the carrot but does not know that the donkey itself is simultaneously moving the carrot further away from itself. The donkey like the rat is being tricked, and Socrates is saying that we are as foolish, in normal life. Why so? There is only an *illusion* of an objective for our actions. There is no *real* objective. For we pursue aims that do not satisfy when they are attained. They satisfy, or seem to satisfy, only when they are *missing*.

---

[1] 218E–219D.

What *exactly* is the problem here? It is that if on Monday you aim to own a horse and on Tuesday own a horse then on Tuesday you will need a further aim or else you will simply quiet down and stop being an agent. Let us say, then, that on Wednesday you form the plan that your horse should win in a horse race and you begin to train it. By Thursday (miraculously) your horse is the champion at the horse races. So what now? Well, again you need a new ideal or you will fall asleep. So what? The problem is that you are always living already in the future, never in the present. You always want what you do *not* have, never what *do* you have. But satisfaction is the same as wanting what you *do* have. More expansively, Socrates is saying that your entire week — or your entire life, really — will consist of bouncing around without an overall strategy or plot. You always want the *next* thing and never what you have *already* got. You never experience satisfaction. You are always already at the horizon in your mind. There is no continuity or core in your life. The self eludes the self!¹

Now, what is the solution to this? We can anticipate this already even though the more complete answer cannot be given until we have looked at Socrates' definitional patterns (in the next section, 2.4).

Here is Socrates (in Plato's *Gorgias*) illustrating the solution by means of examples, after hearing from Callicles that the stronger should get greater shares of goods:

SOCRATES: And ought not the better to have a larger share?

CALLICLES: Not of meats and drinks.

SOCRATES: I understand: then, perhaps, of coats—the skilfullest weaver ought to have the largest coat, and the greatest number of them, and go about clothed in the best and finest of them?

CALLICLES: Fudge about coats!

SOCRATES: Then the skilfullest and best in making shoes ought to have the advantage in shoes; the shoemaker, clearly, should walk about in the largest shoes, and have the greatest number of them?

CALLICLES: Fudge about shoes! What nonsense are you talking?

SOCRATES: Or, if this is not your meaning, perhaps you would say that the wise and good and true husbandman should actually

---

1 The Paradox of Ends is a paradox about *final* causes. Are there analogous paradoxes also for other types of cause, the material, the efficient, and the formal? (On these terms see the Introduction.) Roughly, Zeno's paradoxes in Chapter 1 were about the material, and one of Plato's, in the *Laws*, which discussed in 2.9 below, could be used to formulate a paradox about efficient causes. Kant's paradoxes in Chapter 3 are about efficient, material, and perhaps formal causes, but not about the final, whereas Marx's in Chapter 4 are about the final.

have a larger share of seeds, and have as much seed as possible for his own land?

CALLICLES: How you go on, always talking in the same way, Socrates!

SOCRATES: Yes, Callicles, and also about the same things.

CALLICLES: Yes, by the Gods, you are literally always talking of cobblers and fullers and cooks and doctors, as if this had to do with our argument.

SOCRATES: But why will you not tell me in what a man must be superior and wiser in order to claim a larger share; will you neither accept a suggestion, nor offer one?[1]

Here Socrates is poking fun, to be sure. But that is not all he is doing. He also has a serious point. This is that Callicles should specify both *what rewards* are to be received and what the rewards are to be rewards *for*. If you make coats then your reward should be a coat, or many coats, or a large coat, he is suggesting. If you build houses then you may deserve a house, or a new house, or a solid house, etc. But what Callicles is saying is that the "powerful" — powerful at what? — deserve to have more of, e.g., meat and drinks. Callicles is not saying that the power of the powerful should be *in* producing meats and drinks. It is Socrates who is requiring that. Socrates is requiring that activities and their aims should *fit together*. To speak in a proverb, Socrates is saying that one should reap what one sows. An eye should be taken for an eye, as Hammurabi said. You should use whatever you produce. That is the recipe for independence, autonomy, or freedom.

This is what Socrates is driving at by formulating his main paradox. He is forcing the other speakers to be free. They need to aim at self-sufficiency. The Paradox of Ends points in this direction.

The *Lysis* draws the same moral in different terms. Here Socrates narrates how he questioned a youth named Lysis:

[...] I dare say, Lysis, I said, that your father and mother love you very much.

Certainly, he said.

And they would wish you to be perfectly happy.

Yes.

But do you think that anyone is happy who is in the condition of a slave, and who cannot do what he likes?

I should think not indeed, he said.

---

[1] 490D–491A.

And if your father and mother love you, and desire that you should be happy, no one can doubt that they are very ready to promote your happiness.

Certainly, he replied.

And do they then permit you to do what you like, and never rebuke you or hinder you from doing what you desire?

Yes, indeed, Socrates; there are a great many things which they hinder me from doing.

What do you mean? I said. Do they want you to be happy, and yet hinder you from doing what you like?[1]

Why is this curious? Because happiness seems to be defined as doing what you want. If it does, then it follows that to wish another to be happy is to wish that this other person does what he wants. But things are not thus between Lysis and his parents. They do *not* let him do what he wants, and nonetheless they aim to make him happy.

Socrates continues:

[...] for example, if you want to mount one of your father's chariots, and take the reins at a race, they will not allow you to do so—they will prevent you?

Certainly, he said, they will not allow me to do so.

Whom then will they allow?

There is a charioteer, whom my father pays for driving.

And do they trust a hireling more than you? and may he do what he likes with the horses? and do they pay him for this?

They do.

But I dare say that you may take the whip and guide the mule-cart if you like;—they will permit that?

Permit me! indeed they will not.

Then, I said, may no one use the whip to the mules?

Yes, he said, the muleteer.

And is he a slave or a free man?

A slave, he said.

And do they esteem a slave of more value than you who are their son? And do they entrust their property to him rather than to you? and allow him to do what he likes, when they prohibit you? Answer me now: Are you your own master, or do they not even allow that?

Nay, he said; of course they do not allow it.

Then you have a master?

Yes, my tutor; there he is.

---

[1] 207D–208A.

And is he a slave?

To be sure; he is our slave, he replied.

Surely, I said, this is a strange thing, that a free man should be governed by a slave. And what does he do with you?

He takes me to my teachers.

You do not mean to say that your teachers also rule over you?

Of course they do.

Then I must say that your father is pleased to inflict many lords and masters on you. But at any rate when you go home to your mother, she will let you have your own way, and will not interfere with your happiness; her wool, or the piece of cloth which she is weaving, are at your disposal: I am sure that there is nothing to hinder you from touching her wooden spathe, or her comb, or any other of her spinning implements.

Nay, Socrates, he replied, laughing; not only does she hinder me, but I should be beaten if I were to touch one of them.

Well, I said, this is amazing. And did you ever behave ill to your father or your mother?

No, indeed, he replied.

But why then are they so terribly anxious to prevent you from being happy, and doing as you like?—keeping you all day long in subjection to another, and, in a word, doing nothing which you desire; so that you have no good, as would appear, out of their great possessions, which are under the control of anybody rather than of you, and have no use of your own fair person, which is tended and taken care of by another; while you, Lysis, are master of nobody, and can do nothing?[1]

That is, under what conditions is happiness provided to someone by dominating him?

Why, he said, Socrates, the reason is that I am not of age.

I doubt whether that is the real reason, I said; for I should imagine that your father Democrates, and your mother, do permit you to do many things already, and do not wait until you are of age: for example, if they want anything read or written, you, I presume, would be the first person in the house who is summoned by them.

Very true.

And you would be allowed to write or read the letters in any order which you please, or to take up the lyre and tune the notes, and play with the fingers, or strike with the plectrum, exactly as you please, and neither father nor mother would interfere with you.

---

[1] 208A–209A.

That is true, he said.

Then what can be the reason, Lysis, I said, why they allow you to do the one and not the other?

I suppose, he said, because I understand the one, and not the other.

Yes, my dear youth, I said, the reason is not any deficiency of years, but a deficiency of knowledge; and whenever your father thinks that you are wiser than he is, he will instantly commit himself and his possessions to you.

I think so.[1]

Lysis' parents rule over him, and do not let him do as he wishes, because they wish him to be happy *and* think that he knows too little to make himself happy. If, again, Lysis had knowledge then he could be happy in a self-sufficient way. Then he would not need any masters. He would be his own master.

A few important points are being implied here. One is that happiness does *not* amount to doing what one wants, contra Callicles and Thrasymachus. Happiness amounts rather to doing what you want *if* you know what your happiness requires. Another implied point is that you can be self-sufficient only if you have enough knowledge of some kind. This latter lesson is the decisive one for us.

Now, what *kind* of knowledge yields self-sufficiency? Is Socrates talking about medical knowledge, for example, or about knowledge about philosophy? Or may he mean knowledge about how to run a business? How do we know what he means? This is something he does not explain very plainly in the *Lysis*. But we know, quite clearly, that what he loves and wants are definitions. He seeks them, always. And hence we should not be surprised to hear that Socrates believes there to be a logical pattern for the kind of knowledge that self-sufficiency requires.

But before we come to Socrates' central recipe for happiness and freedom we need to look briefly at what he means to do by means of definitions in general.

2.4 Definitions

Socrates is always after definitions. He is a monomaniac in this way. He is never satisfied with others' interesting examples or stories or suggestive metaphors. He never wants to know whose authority is

---

[1] 209A–209D.

behind a value, if it is not the speaker's own. Why? Why does Socrates require definitions?

He wants people to be as *direct* as possible about values. If you use an example to illustrate a value that you live by then you may be vivid and interesting in doing so but your example will not answer the question what is valuable *in* the example. For typically an example is complex. It has many properties. Which of the properties is central to your evaluation? Is everything about the example as relevant as everything else? Socrates wants speakers to pinpoint what they value precisely. They need to draw limits, as between *Yes* and *No*, or *good* and *bad*. That is why examples will not do. The same problem recurs with stories and metaphors. They are not focused. They say or suggest too many things at once.

But why would one need to be focused?

There is a plain answer to this. Socrates is after the *aims or values* of his interlocutors. Why does this demand definitions? To define something is like drawing a circle around it. It is like saying: "This is *exactly* what it is, and not anything else." Or: "This is the sacred area. *This* I am for. The rest, that is everything outside this, I am *not* for." To define is to be definite. To be definite is to be sharp and complete about an object, and that is to be conscious of it for all that it is. It is to be awake and not sleepy or misty. (Blurred edges would be misty or sleepy.) Now, Socrates' thought is that if you *take aim* then you had better be awake and not sleepy or misty. Why is this? That is just what taking aim is like. It is deliberate, not accidental. There are things that happen to us, as a matter of fate or chance, and then there are things regarding which we take control. And Socrates is all about taking control. He is interested in studying and developing that area of life in which individuals really act — the world of *agents*. He ignores the world of *patients*. He favors the active life, the examined life. He is for "waking up," as we saw, and this means having clear-cut aims.

Here is how he puts this at *Protagoras* 311C–312C:

> Well now, I said, you and I are going to Protagoras, and we are ready to pay him money on your behalf. If our own means are sufficient, and we can gain him with these, we shall be only too glad; but if not, then we are to spend the money of your friends as well. Now suppose, that while we are thus enthusiastically pursuing our object some one were to say to us: Tell me, Socrates, and you Hippocrates, what is Protagoras, and why are you going to pay him money,—how should we answer? I know that Pheidias is a sculptor, and that Homer is a poet; but what appellation is given to Protagoras? how is he designated?

They call him a Sophist, Socrates, he replied.

Then we are going to pay our money to him in the character of a Sophist?

Certainly.

But suppose a person were to ask this further question: And how about yourself? What will Protagoras make of you, if you go to see him?

He answered, with a blush upon his face (for the day was just beginning to dawn, so that I could see him): Unless this differs in some way from the former instances, I suppose that he will make a Sophist of me.

By the gods, I said, and are you not ashamed at having to appear before the Hellenes in the character of a Sophist?

Indeed, Socrates, to confess the truth, I am.

But you should not assume, Hippocrates, that the instruction of Protagoras is of this nature: may you not learn of him in the same way that you learned the arts of the grammarian, or musician, or trainer, not with the view of making any of them a profession, but only as a part of education, and because a private gentleman and freeman ought to know them?

Just so, he said; and that, in my opinion, is a far truer account of the teaching of Protagoras.

I said: I wonder whether you know what you are doing?

And what am I doing?

You are going to commit your soul to the care of a man whom you call a Sophist. And yet I hardly think that you know what a Sophist is; and if not, then you do not even know to whom you are committing your soul and whether the thing to which you commit yourself be good or evil.

Hippocrates wishes to be educated by a "sophist," and to become a "sophist," though he does not know what a "sophist" *is*. Hence he does not know what he is doing, Socrates says. (Hippocrates is shooting in the dark. He does not know what he is after.) But in not knowing what a "sophist" is he cannot *define* "sophist," Socrates makes clear. Yet *if* Hippocrates *could* define "sophist" then Socrates would presumably accept that Hippocrates *does* know what he is doing. (Then it only so happens that "sophist" is *undefinable*, Socrates argues. Sophists are something indefinite. Examined lives cannot be lived with sophisms.)

So now, Socrates wants definitions *and* he wants self-sufficiency. How does he plan to get both of these things together?

2.5 Self-Consistency

Let us proceed in steps, basing on what is already familiar.

As a first step, recall what Heraclitus said in the last chapter, Chapter 1. He was that cryptic and indirect philosopher who did not want to be obvious. But he said, in his strange way, that there is an eternal and divine law in things. This divinity or eternity is not easy to perceive, he said. It comes to us only through wayward routes. Yet we can, as we saw, condense all of this thinking of Heraclitus' to a kind of metaphorical formula, which reads like this:

(i) an ape relates to a man just as a man relates to a god (B 83), that is

(ii) ape: man: god, or

(iii) apeRmanRgod, formally

(iv) aRbRc.

R here stands for relation, as before.

Now (i)–(iv) are not in turn so different, on the *surface*, from

(v) cat: mouse: cheese, that is

(vi) catRmouseRcheese, or — again —

(vii) aRbRc.

But there is an important difference, in that Heraclitus means to communicate to us something that is not familiar or readily perceptible in everyday life, namely what *god* is. We all know what cats and mice and cheese are, so relating them to each other does not really solve any kind of a mystery or fill any kind of a gap. So *that* a:b:c, with cat:mouse:cheese as its contents, tells us nothing new. But this is different in Heraclitus. Heraclitus speaks up at all only so as to say something decisive about an important topic that is normally quite troubling to humans. (His compatriots could deny that god exists, that god can be known, and that god can be spoken of meaningfully at all — just as ours do.) In this general vein, Heraclitus' verbal pattern is in fact a technical or logical invention for speaking intelligibly about something that cannot be spoken about by means of observable examples, such as god. So Heraclitus has found a way for us to talk understandably of things that we do not actually experience! Thus, he offers us an elementary structure for *creative thinking*, nothing less.

How does Heraclitus achieves this? He does not give us only an indirect comparison, like

(viii) cat: mouse: x,

suggesting that x can be filled in with one word or other. (*Cheese* fits the role of x in (viii) but 8 or *treetop* does not.) He does this, yes (because he has his x, as god), but he does more. He also supplies us *degrees* of something. God has *more* of something that man has only some of. Man has a lot of it compared to an ape, but that is not so much compared to what god has. In other words, man is merely ape-like in god-like company.

So Heraclitus' pattern is actually akin to

(ix) 1, 2, 4, 8, and

(x) pretty: prettier: prettiest.

This, too, should sound familiar based on Chapter 1.

Now let us turn to Socrates. In the *Hippias Major* Socrates makes a quick comparison to Heraclitus when he asks one of his definitional questions:

Socrates: "Very well," he will say, "and how about a beautiful lyre? Is it not beautiful?" Shall we agree, Hippias?

Hippias: Yes.

Socrates: After this, then, the man will ask, I am sure, judging by his character: "You most excellent man, how about a beautiful pot? Is it, then, not beautiful?"

Hippias: Socrates, who is the fellow? What an uncultivated person, who has the face to mention such worthless things in a dignified discussion !

Socrates: That's the kind of person he is, Hippias, not elegant, but vulgar, thinking of nothing but the truth. But nevertheless the man must be answered, and I will declare my opinion beforehand: if the pot were made by a good potter, were smooth and round and well fired, as are some of the two-handled pots, those that hold six choes, very beautiful ones — if that were the kind of pot he asked about, we must agree that it is beautiful; for how could we say that being beautiful it is not beautiful?

Hippias: We could not at all, Socrates.

Socrates: "Then," he will say, "a beautiful pot also is beautiful, is it not?" Answer.

Hippias: Well, Socrates, it is like this, I think. This utensil, when well wrought, is beautiful, but absolutely considered it does not deserve to be regarded as beautiful in comparison with a mare and a maiden and all the beautiful things.

Socrates: Very well I understand, Hippias, that the proper reply to him who asks these questions is this: "Sir, you are not aware that the saying of Heraclitus is good, that 'the most beautiful of monkeys is ugly compared with the race of man,' and the most beautiful of pots is ugly compared with the race of maidens, as Hippias the wise man says." Is it not so, Hippias?

Hippias: Certainly, Socrates; you replied rightly.

Socrates: Listen then. For I am sure that after this he will say: "Yes, but, Socrates, if we compare maidens with gods, will not the same thing happen to them that happened to pots when compared with maidens? Will not the most beautiful maiden appear ugly? Or does not Heraclitus, whom you cite, mean just this, that the wisest of men, if compared with a god, will appear a monkey, both in wisdom and in beauty and in everything else?" Shall we agree, Hippias, that the most beautiful maiden is ugly if compared with the gods?

Hippias: Yes, for who would deny that, Socrates?

Socrates: If, then, we agree to that, he will laugh and say: "Socrates, do you remember the question you were asked?" "I do," I shall say, "the question was what the absolute beautiful is." "Then," he will say, "when you were asked for the beautiful, do you give as your reply what is, as you yourself say, no more beautiful than ugly?" "So it seems," I shall say; or what do you, my friend, advise me to say?

Hippias: That is what I advise; for, of course, in saying that the human race is not beautiful in comparison with gods, you will be speaking the truth.

Socrates: "But if I had asked you," he will say, "in the beginning what is beautiful and ugly, if you had replied as you now do, would you not have replied correctly? But do you still think that the absolute beautiful, by the addition of which all other things are adorned and made to appear beautiful, when its form is added to any of them — do you think that is a maiden or a mare or a lyre?"

Hippias: Well, certainly, Socrates, if that is what he is looking for, nothing is easier than to answer and tell him what the beautiful is, by which all other things are adorned and by the addition of which they are made to appear beautiful. So the fellow is very simple-minded and knows nothing about beautiful possessions. For if you reply to him: "This that you ask about, the beautiful, is nothing else but gold," he will be thrown into confusion and will not attempt to confute you. For we all know, I fancy, that wherever this is added, even what before appears ugly will appear beautiful when adorned with gold.[1]

At first, in this passage, Socrates seems to be asking for an ordinary definition of beauty. There are many ordinary examples of beauty, he and Hippias agree, but Socrates does not want the ordinary examples. He wants something more. If he sought a customary definition then he would have it as the property, or the list of properties, that is common and specific to all and only beautiful examples. But Socrates is not after this kind of a definition, for two reasons. The first reason

---

[1] 288C–289E.

is that he introduces degrees of satisfaction, like Heraclitus. Hence some things are more beautiful than others. This thought of hierarchy does not belong at all to the ordinary thought of a definition. In an ordinary definition one says what it takes to belong to a group, and what suffices for belonging to it, nothing more. The members of the group are all equal. There is no hierarchy then. The second reason that Socrates goes beyond the limits of a normal definition is that he "self-predicates," saying that whatever is the standard of beauty must itself be the most beautiful thing.[1] This second thing is something Heraclitus did not say, so here he goes beyond Heraclitus as well. But this is the most important thing in Socrates altogether.

Notice the difference. If in Heraclitus we have:

(xi) aRbRc, namely as
(xii) ape: man: god,
then in Socrates we have:
(xiii) aRbRR, i.e.
(xiv) a golden spoon is less beautiful than Helen who is less beautiful than beauty itself.

How is Socrates' formula different from Heraclitus'? A first difference is that Socrates condenses Heraclitus' formula by using less symbols. This is because for Socrates c = R, whereas in Heraclitus c ≠ R. So Socrates' thinking is more compact. A second difference is that Socrates' formula is self-relational. Heraclitus' formula would be self-relational as well if *god* communicated Heraclitus' formula to us. But we hear it from Heraclitus, and Heraclitus is a *man*, and in Heraclitus man is only a middle term, like b in a: b: c. Put differently, what Heraclitus' expression *points towards* is not the producer or the production of that expression. It points *beyond* itself. It is *not* self-contained, and it is not self-sufficient.

Now we have specified how it is possible to provide a self-relation. The reader knows how self-relations can be generated. Simultaneously, this is to grasp how there are selves in Socrates' dialectic. The selves are things which relate, and what they relate to are themselves. Every self is a relation to a relation. All one needs for this kind of self-sufficiency is (xiii) above.

In (xiii), whatever relation one takes should be reproduced on the object–level. For R is not a link between terms like a and b: R is, in (xiii), *itself* also a term, i.e., a linked and not only a link. Why is this? Because this is self-consistent. This is to be in harmony with oneself.

---

[1] For some standard views on self-predication see Nehamas.

This is to reap what one sows. The great value of all reasoning and logic is consistency, and the only evil by the same standards is inconsistency or contradiction. Socrates' dialectical ideal is only a particularly strong version of consistency. This is the soul he wants to tend to. It is all about harmony, which is but a softer word for logical consistency. So here, in the end, is the reason why he wants individuals to develop the dialectical skills of respectful questioning and to confront paradoxes and produce self-predicated definitions.

This should not be an entirely surprising result, given that we already sketched several different self-relations in the Introduction. We then saw what form they have. It is aRbRc...zRz or else aRbRc... zRR. It is this second version that we have now deciphered form the *Hippias Major*. (One should not be led astray by the fact that the same logical pattern can be communicated with fewer or more several terms. Essentially speaking aRbRc...zRR and aRbRR say exactly the same thing.)

What should also ring a bell is the kinship of the preceding imagery of Socrates with R6, that is, the dialectic of the "formal cause," as Aristotle called it. This dialectic moves from chaos to order, or verbally from metaphors through contradictions to self-definitions. This is exactly what Socrates provides. How so? Well, he begins his dialogues by finding examples and metaphors and then he moves to paradoxes, such as the Paradox of Ends, and then finally he requires a self-relational definition. This is just one version of R6, a linguistic version.

There are a few questions one may feel it necessary to raise at this point. The first is, how can Socrates possibly desire a mere definition as the *hallmark* of self-sufficiency? How could a formula possibly take care of something as large as positive freedom or self-knowledge? Is self-sufficiency not something much more than a mere pattern of thought? The reply is that if we want to see validity in Socrates' dialectic as it is, that is without adding anything of our own to it, then we should conclude that Socrates is actually after *intellectual* self-sufficiency as an end. In other words, he philosophizes because he wants to *liberate thought*. This is how his procedure makes coherent sense. The implication is then that he is really not after the kind of independence that, say, Jefferson's self-fed farmers have, or the sort of independence a nation state can aspire to. But we should not rush from this to the conclusion that Socrates is necessarily mistaken in focusing so much on thought. For there is an advantage to his kind of dialectic. That advantage is, unsurprisingly, definiteness. Socratic independence, the independence of the free thinker, is clear cut. We cannot say quite the same of yeoman farmers and countries. They are complex and, by comparison, rather messy affairs to deal with. They are much harder to measure. For definitions we have clear-cut criteria so we can be quite sharp in operating with them. Socratic independence is *purer*, logically and metaphysically.

A second question one might raise now is whether Socrates' dialectic is not something quite *rigid*. For who would ever be happy with mere definitions? Perhaps thoughts can be made logically sharp, and perhaps it is true that one can be highly self-consistent in one's imagination, but what is that supposed to count for, in the real world? Is the world not full of all kinds of interesting physical and empirical and emotional phenomena? Are we really to avoid them all? Who could follow Socrates to his clinical place of rational thoughts and really be happy? This way to question Socrates' dialectic is misled because Socrates never takes an interlocutor *directly* to the techniques of definitions, for he wants the definitional quest of free and rational thought to have *real life bearings*. The only way he gets such weights in, however, and the only manner in which the emotions and imaginations of his interlocutors are also addressed in his essentially logical process, is by beginning not from definitions but from metaphorical and mythical values. But this is what he *does*, dialogue in and dialogue out. This is how he captures the hearts of men, and not only their minds. In the second phase of Socrates' process we have paradoxes, which we have already studied in this chapter; and then thirdly we have definitions. The paradoxes are important too, because like all tools of indirect methods paradoxes and problems activate and stimulate minds. So the liberating process moves *from* metaphoring and paradoxes *to* self-definitions. It is not a location but a process. This is why the gadfly Socrates can authentically claim to wake real people up. He *engages* the rude Callicles and Thrasymachus, the young Lysis, the boastful Hippias, etc. He does not look away from all the complications of life: he looks *inside* them.[1]

---

[1] In aRbRR a happens first, then R, then b, etc. This is a *temporal* series of events or acts. Dialectics are like that. They are not unchanging states; they are changing processes.
Also notice that the series of events cannot be *repetitive*. If one ends in a definition then one begins from metaphors and contradictions, for example — not from definitions. If one ended where one began then one could not advance or inform anyone; but in a dialectic one always discovers, creates, reveals, liberates, etc. (I am ignoring the possibility of a surprising return. For example, in the slogan "No means no!" the import is that "No" really does mean "No." It does not really mean "Maybe," as it does in Voltaire's quip that if a lady says 'no' she means 'maybe,' and if she says 'maybe' she means 'yes,' and if she says 'yes,' she

A third question we can deal with very briefly. This is whether Socrates can have a self-predicated standard and still *seek* self-sufficiency or self-knowledge. Has he not already attained it in his self-predicated formula? And is he therefore not only pretending and being ironic in saying that he wishes to *learn* from his interlocutors? Is he not really only teaching, no matter how indirectly? In reply, this question is premised on a mistake. For to have a criterion for one's aim is not yet to possess the aim. Socrates' questions and demands ultimately have a self-predicated structure, this is true, but this structure is to be *instanced*, or exemplified, by something his interlocutors say and value. The whole point of having the criterion is to aid the search — or indeed to make the search possible at all, as we will see in the next section. Metaphorically, all Socrates has is a map. He is looking for a place that will match this map. The map by itself does not count for much. His logical standard is a mere map until some real personality comes along to match with it.[1]

2.6 Innateness

Socrates teaches in the ways that we have described, and then the Athenians have him killed for it. Plato, like so many other young men, walks around in Athens and follows Socrates, paying close attention to everything he says and does. It is as if Plato saw some kind of a savior in Socrates. He writes Socrates' conversations down, more or less *verbatim*. But then, once Socrates has died, Plato does not stop writing. He first stays rather close to Socrates' ways of thought but with time he ranges further and further. He begins to invent things which Socrates might say, or could say, if things were carried further. Thereby he fashions his own fictional "Socrates."

This fictional "Socrates" speaks only for Plato's own philosophy. Plato's philosophy remains dialectical, but what typifies it is its

is not a lady. The slogan which seems tautological, "No means no!," is actually informative if the hearer is possessed by Voltaire's prejudice.)
[1] There is very little direct information in Socrates about what exactly can turn out to be self-predicated. He often begins his dialectical processes from metaphors from poems, seeking to derive an instructive content from these. He does not begin from dreams. (If he did he would be more like a psychoanalyst than a literary theorist.) A further option would be to compare, with Heraclitus, childhood and adulthood, given that children often seem to wonder about particulars and have difficulties producing generalized laws or formulae, while adults are capable of generalizing but not of wondering. Socrates would then be a kind of gateway from the curiosities of childhood to the responsibilities of adulthood. (Compare my *Socrates' Criteria*, Chapters 2 and 3, for further alternatives.)

overwhelming ambition. Plato wants to draw much more out of dialectics than Socrates did. Plato wants to prove the soul's immortality, a valid political utopia, God's reality, and more. *Meno* is the dialogue which begins this phase of philosophical megalomania, so we will look at it first. It is our gateway to Plato's dialectics.[1]

There is a paradox in the *Meno* that resembles the *Lysis'* and the *Gorgias'* Paradox of Ends, and in reply to this paradox Plato begins to fashion his bold theory of innate knowledge, which he then combines with our supposed ability to recollect metaphysically and, in the *Phaedo*, to live eternally, to know God, etc. What is this new paradox?

> MENO: And how will you enquire, Socrates, into that which you do not know? What will you put forth as the subject of enquiry? And if you find what you want, how will you ever know that this is the thing which you did not know?
>
> SOCRATES: I know, Meno, what you mean; but just see what a tiresome dispute you are introducing. You argue that a man cannot enquire either about that which he knows, or about that which he does not know; for if he knows, he has no need to enquire; and if not, he cannot; for he does not know the very subject about which he is to enquire.
>
> MENO: Well, Socrates, and is not the argument sound?
>
> SOCRATES: I think not.
>
> MENO: Why not?
>
> SOCRATES: I will tell you why: I have heard from certain wise men and women who spoke of things divine that—
>
> MENO: What did they say?
>
> SOCRATES: They spoke of a glorious truth, as I conceive.
>
> MENO: What was it? and who were they?
>
> SOCRATES: Some of them were priests and priestesses, who had studied how they might be able to give a reason of their profession: there have been poets also, who spoke of these things by inspiration, like Pindar, and many others who were inspired. And they say—mark, now, and see whether their words are true—they say that the soul of man is immortal, and at one time has an end, which is termed dying, and at another time is born again, but is never destroyed. And the moral is, that a man ought to live always in perfect holiness. 'For in the ninth year Persephone sends the souls of those from whom she has received the penalty of ancient crime back again from beneath

---

[1] The *Meno* is often categorized as a transitional dialogue, for its "Socrates" is a mix between the historically real Socrates and Plato's fictional "Socrates" (see Fine vol. 1 p. 1). I will treat it as Plato's creation, to play it safe.

into the light of the sun above, and these are they who become noble kings and mighty men and great in wisdom and are called saintly heroes in after ages.' The soul, then, as being immortal, and having been born again many times, and having seen all things that exist, whether in this world or in the world below, has knowledge of them all; and it is no wonder that she should be able to call to remembrance all that she ever knew about virtue, and about everything; for as all nature is akin, and the soul has learned all things; there is no difficulty in her eliciting or as men say learning, out of a single recollection all the rest, if a man is strenuous and does not faint; for all enquiry and all learning is but recollection.[1]

Meno says here that it is impossible to inquire into something one does not know, because one would not recognize the sought object if one came by it. Inquiring into what one already knows, however, would of course be pointless. So it seems that one must either drift aimlessly or stay put, not inquiring. Either way forward movements appear impossible. It is as if one could not learn on purpose. This is the Paradox of Inquiry.

Is there an error in this? Plato's "Socrates" in this passage seems not to think so. For his reply is that no progressive movement is needed. He is for staying put! This is what his claim to innateness amounts to. (One should only stay in "perfect holiness," above.)

Before examining Plato's theory of innate knowledge in more detail we need to note why the real, historical Socrates of the earlier Platonic dialogues, whom we have already gotten to know earlier in this chapter, would not seem to go along with Plato.

The real Socrates would defend the possibility of progressive inquiry. How do we know? He holds that one can, and should, seek self-knowledge and self-predication, and these require progression. That is, Socrates holds that one can aim at a full independence which one does not yet have. How? Crucially, Socrates distinguishes between the *formal* features of his aim and the aim *itself*. One can know the form or structure of the aim in advance of attaining that aim. Moreover, the form or structure suffices for the purpose of recognizing the aim. Hence we know that it is not the case, for Socrates, that one knows how to recognize the aim only once one has attained it. There is no circle because structural abstraction is possible. One can think ahead and plan ahead.[2]

---

[1] 80D–81D. A similar paradox appears at *Euthydemus* 275D–278C, perhaps suggesting that this paradox is only a well-known sophism at the time and not Plato's or Socrates' innovation.

[2] What is this form that Socrates goes by? aRbRR, as above.

Perhaps it will help if this is phrased more vividly. Socrates' view is that one can construct a map for a region, let us say for the country of Wonderland, in advance of visiting Wonderland. Therefore, if one came by Wonderland then one would know that one is there. But one does not need to be *in* Wonderland to possess the map, or to construct the map. Most importantly of all, because one can make the map without being in the country one can *search* for the country.

Now, the paradox of the *Meno*, cited above, arises only on the condition that one can *not* have the map before one is in the country. For only then will it be true to say that, e.g., Wonderland cannot be sought. If Wonderland is recognized only from *inside* Wonderland, then no one can possibly ever find his or her way to Wonderland.

How is it possible to construct a map of Wonderland without having visited the place? Is this not an unrealistic assumption? It is realistic for a very simple reason: the Wonderland of Socrates is an *ideal* place, not a real one. He has a map of a place in which he *would* be free and self-knowing, *if* he were there. He is not there, and he has never been there. He is looking for the place.

How, then, does Socrates know which features Wonderland must have? Because his "Wonderland" is a place in which there is self-knowledge or self-predication. He knows what those are, formally, so he can draw a map of his Wonderland.

But how does Socrates know what self-knowledge or self-predication is like? Or how does he know that he should go to a place where they are? Why is *his* Wonderland *the* Wonderland, or the wonder of wonders, or that for which all free-thinking agents should aim? He knows this because self-relational definitions solve the Paradox of Ends, from the *Lysis* and the *Gorgias*, which again are the paradoxes which threaten all free agents with aimlessness.

All of this is only to rephrase from the previous sections. Socrates can sincerely approach Hippias and Lysis and Callicles, etc., in his search for his final answer because he has his formal map in his hands.

How different, then, is Meno's paradox from Socrates' paradoxes in the *Lysis* and the *Gorgias*? They are very different, in that Meno formulates a paradox that is avoidable without much ado, whereas Socrates' paradoxes are hard and demand specific responses. One could avoid Meno's paradox also without developing any formal map for aims. One could say, like a biologist, that one is looking for a tiger. If the biologist knows in advance that the tiger will have the properties xyz and xyz suffice for the recognition of tigers then the biologist can search the jungle happily and there is no paradox. The biologist need not be a formalist like Socrates. Searching and inquiring are possible in many ways that are not like Socrates'. You can look for your watch because you know what it looks like though you do not know where it is, etc.

This should now be clear.

But Plato does *not* see things in this way, as we noted. For he develops a theory of *innateness* to avoid Meno's paradox. What is innateness?

If we have innate knowledge then we know things without being taught those things. We will not even need to be given any conclusive evidence for them! And we will not need to have pondered them before, so they can be utterly unfamiliar to us before we come to them. And yet we will simply know them. How? We are born with the knowledge, Plato says. That is one of his big ideas.[1]

The *Meno* makes innateness a vivid phenomenon by describing how even an uneducated slave boy has it. The boy does not respond to questions correctly all the time. But he makes just the kinds of right leaps and guesses which support the innateness hypothesis.

Now let us look at a passage from the *Meno* in which the slave boy is not talking. (This is clearer about the logical pieces that Plato's theory of innateness requires.) In this passage Plato's "Socrates" and Meno discuss a fundamental aspect of innate knowledge:

SOCRATES: To what then do we give the name of figure? Try and answer. Suppose that when a person asked you this question either about figure or colour, you were to reply, Man, I do not understand what you want, or know what you are saying; he would look rather astonished and say: Do you not understand that I am looking for the 'simile in multis'? And then he might put the question in another form: Meno, he might say, what is that 'simile in multis' which you call figure, and which includes not only round and straight figures, but all? Could you not answer that question, Meno? I wish that you would try; the attempt will be good practice with a view to the answer about virtue.

MENO: I would rather that you should answer, Socrates.

SOCRATES: Shall I indulge you?

MENO: By all means.

SOCRATES: And then you will tell me about virtue?

MENO: I will.

SOCRATES: Then I must do my best, for there is a prize to be won.

---

[1] Compare Chomsky for a recent theory of innate knowledge. Between Plato and Chomsky one finds such "innatists" as Descartes and Kant.

MENO: Certainly.

SOCRATES: Well, I will try and explain to you what figure is. What do you say to this answer?—Figure is the only thing which always follows colour. Will you be satisfied with it, as I am sure that I should be, if you would let me have a similar definition of virtue?

MENO: But, Socrates, it is such a simple answer.

SOCRATES: Why simple?

MENO: Because, according to you, figure is that which always follows colour.

SOCRATES: Granted.

MENO: But if a person were to say that he does not know what colour is, any more than what figure is—what sort of answer would you have given him?

SOCRATES: I should have told him the truth. And if he were a philosopher of the eristic and antagonistic sort, I should say to him: You have my answer, and if I am wrong, your business is to take up the argument and refute me. But if we were friends, and were talking as you and I are now, I should reply in a milder strain and more in the dialectician's vein; that is to say, I should not only speak the truth, but I should make use of premises which the person interrogated would be willing to admit. And this is the way in which I shall endeavour to approach you. You will acknowledge, will you not, that there is such a thing as an end, or termination, or extremity?—all which words I use in the same sense, although I am aware that Prodicus might draw distinctions about them: but still you, I am sure, would speak of a thing as ended or terminated—that is all which I am saying—not anything very difficult.

MENO: Yes, I should; and I believe that I understand your meaning.

SOCRATES: And you would speak of a surface and also of a solid, as for example in geometry.

MENO: Yes.

SOCRATES: Well then, you are now in a condition to understand my definition of figure. I define figure to be that in which the solid ends; or, more concisely, the limit of solid.

MENO: And now, Socrates, what is colour?[1]

One can be taught what a figure is if one knows what a color is, "Socrates" — that is, Plato — is saying. The point is that one can be informed of something new on the basis of what one already knows. How is this possible? Well, the old and familiar elements can be re-

---

combined into a new whole. To use Hume's classic example, you can construct a gold mountain in your imagination because gold and mountains are something familiar to you from experience. You need not be familiar with gold mountains. You need not have seen any of them. You need the *parts* to be familiar, and on their basis the whole can be unfamiliar and novel. But you can readily imagine this new whole and communicate it to others. It is intelligible though it is new. You merely recombine the old parts. That is one way to be creative.

You can also go further in the same direction, of course. You may add that the mountain is shaped like a lion. You can go as far as your vocabulary of elements allows. You can make the mountain old, high, whatever. If you have a rich vocabulary then you can go further and further in your fiction, and everyone with the same basic vocabulary will be able to follow you.

What happens if your repertoire is poor? If you had, say, only the colors black and white to work with then all you could produce would be shades of grey. You could still move around some, as you could still make many different mixtures and hence many different shades; but your possibilities would be comparatively limited.

It is important to notice that whatever vocabulary one has, rich or poor, one faces certain logical limits. For even if you can create by recombining elements, you cannot make inconsistent combinations. For instance a gold mountain that is spiritual would not make sense, if gold is material. Your new whole would be unintelligible, to you and to all hearers. But this limitation still leaves you with a great deal of space to move in, of course. You get unicorns, Wonderlands, and so many other things. And this is how Plato proposes to explain geometric figures as well as the essence of virtue in the previous excerpt. One needs only "limit," "color," etc., and one gets, say, points and lines and circles and squares, etc. One just combines the old parts in new wholes.

Next, we can *reverse* this image and consider how novel *abstractions* can be produced, for this is closer to what Socrates and Plato try to in their dialectical philosophies. Just as we can *combine* elements to form complexes, as above, we can also *break down* complexes into elements we had not thought of before. We build or break up, add or subtract. Both are pathways to novel thought-products.

Let us take an example. If you had only shades of grey you might be able to separate from those shades a darkest black and a brightest white. Now you would be working in the general direction of Socrates and Plato. Similarly, if you had come across some gold rings and golden curls, and also with some gold spoons, you might distinguish a concept of gold that is common and specific to all of the cases you have met with, as it were tearing the concept away from the individual rings, curls, and spoons. You would be abstracting. Also compare:

the shadow of a cloud.

ape R man R x.

the rich without their money.

In these cases one separates and distinguishes, taking smaller things out of bigger things.

In principle a dialectician could use either model to produce definitions, the one in which one adds or the one in which one subtracts. Accordingly dialecticians can move in time to novel expressions that are either increasingly complex or increasingly simple. If we move far enough then we may or may not reach some kind of limit or self-relation. If we reach the self-relation then we complete the dialectical pattern. If we do not we have only a kind of half-dialectic or quasi-dialectic, and not a real one. (This should be understandable based on the Introduction.)

Now what is supposed to be *innate* in this? We have one story about this from Plato another story from Socrates. Before coming to Plato's let me say a few brief things about Socrates'.

Socrates' story is really only a *tacit* story, because he does not actually discuss innateness. We can tell that his dialectic implies some things about innateness even if he does not draw the implications in what he says. Here is one such implication. If one seeks, and tells others to seek, *self-knowledge*, as Socrates does in 2.1, then one needs to believe in the existence of innate characters in all the seekers. Conversely, if all our basic properties were learned from our environments then we could not seek self-knowledge (not even about our characters as learners, for on a fully consistent theory even *those* characters would be learned from environments!). So Socrates must rely on innateness in some version. We need to have selves to find or Socrates' quest for self-knowledge does not make sense.[1]

Now let us turn to Plato. What is his view of innateness? He says that one needs first of all to operate in a dialectic that moves from

---

[1] On the other hand, we are not entitled to attribute any very bold theory of innateness to Socrates. For he clearly needs to explain his formal ideals at length to his interlocutors and they fail to understand him so often that one suspects that the formalities are not innate, or at least that if they are innate then they are concealed deep inside the interlocutors' subconscious minds. Hippias is all at sea about self-predication in the *Hippias Major*, and Ion does not understand even the most elementary definitional norms in the *Ion*, etc. Compare Beversluis and Santas.

complexes to simples, not vice versa.[1] Then the extreme simples, which one may eventually come by if one practices dialectics well enough, and which all along are the aims of inquiry, are innate.[2] But this already takes us to the next section and the next dialogue: the *Phaedo*.

2.7 Immortality

With the *Phaedo* we approach the Platonic heartland. Now the historical Socrates has already fallen far behind and Plato's ambitions are very bold indeed.

In the *Phaedo* Plato argues that we actually know that our souls or psyches are immortal. Our bodies will die, but not our souls. Why, exactly? Here is the central argument:

"Do you not know, then, that lovers when they see a lyre, or a garment, or any thing else which their favorite is accustomed to use, are thus affected; they both recognize the lyre, and receive in their minds the form of the person to whom the lyre belonged? This is reminiscence: just as anyone, seeing Simmias, is often reminded of Cebes, and so in an infinite number of similar instances."

"An infinite number, indeed, by Jupiter!" said Simmias.

"Is not, then," he said, "something of this sort a kind of reminiscence, especially when one is thus affected with respect to things which, from lapse of time, and not thinking of them, one has now forgotten?"

"Certainly," he replied.

"But what?" he continued. "Does it happen that when one sees a painted horse or a painted lyre one is reminded of a man, and that when one sees a picture of Simmias one is reminded of Cebes?"

"Certainly."

"And does it not also happen that on seeing a picture of Simmias one is reminded of Simmias himself?"

"It does, indeed," he replied.

---

[1] Who proceeds vice versa? I.e., which dialectician aims at vast complexes? Hegel. In Plato a dialectic is like a tree which begins from a trunk and then develops smaller and smaller branches. It is about division or separation. The smallest parts are the Forms. In Hegel the opposite happens, so the image is like of a system of rivers. Smaller rivers flow in time to larger ones and ultimately all of the rivers flow into one ocean, so there is more and more unity. On Hegel, see Horstmann and Charles Taylor. On this aspect of Plato see Silverman.

[2] Someone other than Plato might answer this question differently. Chomsky, for example, takes certain grammatical rules to be innate. These are not the smallest combinable elements but the rules of combination. Speakers know, on an innate basis, what to put together with what. Because speakers have similar knowledge they can communicate with each other.

"Does it not happen, then, according to all this, that reminiscence arises partly from things like, and partly from things unlike?"

"It does."

"But when one is reminded by things like, is it not necessary that one should be thus further affected, so as to perceive whether, as regards likeness, this falls short or not of the thing of which one has been reminded?"

"It is necessary," he replied.

"Consider, then," said Socrates, "if the case is thus. Do we allow that there is such a thing as equality? I do not mean of one log with another, nor one stone with another, nor any thing else of this kind, but something altogether different from all these—abstract equality; do we allow that there is any such thing, or not?"

"By Jupiter! we most assuredly do allow it," replied Simmias.

"And do we know what it is itself?"

"Certainly," he replied.

"Whence have we derived the knowledge of it? Is it not from the things we have just now mentioned, and that from seeing logs, or stones, or other things of the kind, equal, we have from these formed an idea of that which is different from these—for does it not appear to you to be different? Consider the matter thus. Do not stones that are equal, and logs sometimes that are the same, appear at one time equal, and at another not?"

"Certainly."

"But what? Does abstract equality ever appear to you unequal? or equality inequality?"

"Never, Socrates, at any time."

"These equal things, then," he said, "and abstract equality, are not the same?"

"By no means, Socrates, as it appears."[1]

This passage says that often one is reminded of something by what it is not identical with or equal to. One remembers a person after seeing a lyre or a garment, for example. One does not remember only a lyre or a garment after seeing a lyre or a garment, so one does not ordinarily spin in circles. One leaps beyond the stimulants. One recalls more than one really has evidence for, before one's eyes. In other words, one's mind is active.

But then this same passage goes on to say something more puzzling. The *relation* of equality should be familiar to us from somewhere. But it is not familiar to us from our ordinary experiences. We do not meet

---

[1] 73D–74C.

with equal relations between sticks and stones, for example, but only with approximations of equal relations. The sticks and the stones are not exactly equal, only somewhat so. And this leaves us only with the alternative that we must have met with equal relations before we came to this place in which we have all these experiences with mere sticks and stones, Plato says. We must know the perfect case from somewhere because we think by means of it. We could not possibly have thoughts of perfection, he means, unless we had met with something perfect somewhere already.

But what Plato really wants to say is something deeper. We met the Form of the Equal before we were born. Therefore, we lived somewhere else before we came into these bodies, and to this place with mere sticks and stones. Our ideas are just too perfect for this complex world. We belong, in fact, to a much simpler place in which there is no birth or death at all. That is where we were before we came into this material world, and that is where we will go back when our bodies die! There, in that abstract heaven, we never have any experiences. There we have only the pure Forms and us as souls, forever. *We are immortal*, as souls.

To continue a little on this deeper level, Plato's argument seems at first to be about the Forms but really it is about us. It appears to be about memories of the Forms, but more than that, it is about memories of *ourselves*. For it is the immortality of souls that the *Phaedo* attempts to prove. That is what this whole dialogue is about, and the above excerpt is only one of so many routes by which Plato tries to arrive at that conclusion. The eternity of the Ideas or Forms is only a means to that aim. In other words, the *Phaedo* is mainly about remembering our own earlier spiritual existence!

Nonetheless the technical argument of the above passage focuses on the Forms, not on our souls. It says the Form of Equality is something separate and abstract. Also, this Form is self-predicated, in the already familiar sense. For the Equal is a measure for things which measure is also, at the same time, perfectly satisfied only by that same measure. The yard-stick is itself the only perfectly yard-long thing there is, as it were.

Logically the point is exactly as it was in the *Hippias Major*. For in this new excerpt the relation of equality is said to be instanced only imperfectly between sticks and stones. They are somewhat equal but not exactly. Exact equality, however, or Equality as a Form, can be met with only in the abstract, and ultimately it must be a relation of an abstraction to itself. This time Plato's sequence of terms can seem to consist really of pairs, as in $a: b:: c: d$. For a low-level pair instances a relation imperfectly and the high-level one does it perfectly, and there seems to be a pair of pairs. But actually the *relations* now are viewed as primary, and not any pairs, for if the Equal is one then it cannot be a pair except of terms or symbols. For being one, or equal to itself, it is not two things. So we have a rather straight-forward self-predication once more, and the complication is only superficial. (The use of pairs results in no important change.)[1]

But if the formal basis is so similar in Plato's *Phaedo* to what it was in Socrates' *Hippias Major*, are the arguments drawn from that formal pattern also similar? Not at all.

We saw already that even the issue of innateness, as it arose in the *Meno*, was no longer Socrates' concern, and the claim of the soul's immortality is something much more radical than that. Why was the innateness thesis not Socrates'? Socrates focused on ethics. Innate knowledge is an epistemological topic. It is the kind of theme that will interest a more theoretic person. It would interest Thales, who, according the Plato's *Theaetetus*, marvels at the skies so much that he does not notice where he steps and falls into a ditch! That is not the fate of a man like Socrates. Socrates is not interested in theorizing impractical things. He is centered on what must be done now. Which direction is forward?, he demands. He is impatient. He cannot listen to long speeches. Things must be shown quickly or he will move on. His existential imperative is urgent.[2]

Plato, in the *Phaedo*, is far away from Socrates. There is a different ambition. It is no longer purely ethical; it is metaphysical. What does this difference mean?

---

[1] If Equality is a paradigmatic Form in the *Phaedo* then it is reasonable to take that dialogue's Forms as *relations*. This fits well with dialectics, because dialectica are relational processes.
Equality is in a sense *the* relation, and perhaps the philosophically most puzzling one, because it identifies what it concerns without simply copying it. This is what concerns Frege as well. If I identify the morning star as Venus then I am not simply repeating that the morning star is the morning star. Rather, I am providing new information. If I equate, or if I identify, or if I explain a meaning, etc., then I am saying the *same* thing twice, or talking about the same thing twice, *but* as time passes I talk in a more revealing way. So there is a repetition but also an advance. (For Frege, the "reference" stays the same while the "sense" evolves.) All of Plato's descriptions of the Forms do not accord with this relational view. For example in the *Republic* (596A) the Forms seem to correspond to universals. There is a Form unique to beds, maybe to mice, perhaps to piles, etc. Plato seems to change his mind. For an argument that Plato does this see my *Socrates' Criteria*, Chapters 7 and 8. The opposite view is that of the Tübingen School, which holds that Plato has a hidden center that is changeless (see Krämer).
[2] I take the phrase "existental imperative" from Magnus.

Socrates, as he appears in Plato's early dialogues, cares only for instructions how one ought to think and live. He does not care how things *are already*. He is not interested in the orbits of the stars or the normal rise and fall of empires. He wants only to find how to live a life that is properly examined, or holy, etc. In contrast, the "Socrates" of Plato's middle and later dialogues, who is not the historically real Socrates anymore but Plato's fiction, *does* care about reality. The *Phaedo* goes into self-predication only so as to show that our souls are immortal! The question about values is no longer the aim. It has become a means. Ethics has come to serve religion. Socrates was different: he brushed religion aside, to make room for ethics. So there is really a sea change between Socrates and Plato.

From a technically philosophical angle the difference between Socrates and Plato boils down to a difference about the *reality* of the Forms or Ideas. Both predicate value of the Forms or Ideas, but Socrates does not care whether they are real. Plato does. Plato argues many times that the Forms or Ideas are something simple and abstract that will exist forever, and that have always existed.

Plato's metaphysical thinking is easiest to understand by thinking of a mathematical point. If you draw a point on paper then, for the point to be visible to you, you cannot have the point be extensionless. If you zoomed in on your drawing with a microscope you would find that it has the width, say, of half a millimeter. But a mathematical point is extensionless. It is not even half a millimeter in length, because it has *no* length. It is a *point*. It has one exact location. It is not a colored circle that covers some area. But do you think you can draw an extensionless point that you can see? Of course you cannot. The only shapes you will ever see have extensions. They must spread out at least somewhat or you will not spot them. That is just the way your senses work. Now, metaphysical Platonism says that the point is a real abstraction. You "get" what it is, though you never see it on paper (or on a computer screen, or in drawings on the sand, etc.). The mathematical point is alike to equality in this respect. Again similarly, take a triangle. You never meet with the perfect triangle, that is the triangle with *exactly* straight lines and even angles. But that perfect triangle is what all the triangles of the world are modeled on. It is the "mathematical" triangle, which you can define though you cannot see it. In general, such perfect, abstract, eternal things that you "get" are the Forms or Ideas. They are the models for all rational thought, Plato says. They are like landmarks on a map we use to make sense of things and to make our plans. Or, to vary the metaphor, they are like blueprints in heaven for how good thinking is done anywhere at any time. Again in different terms, they are archetypes. They are pure and simple, and everything else follows them and mixes them and deviates from their simple perfection. The mixtures arise in time and break up into their smallest parts again, and so there is birth and death; but the smallest parts remain all the while, so they are eternal. They never break. Nothing can destroy them.

Plato's metaphysical thinking is not silly. There is a long tradition of Platonic metaphysics that continues to this day, especially in the philosophy of logic and mathematics. In ethics and aesthetics the tradition has been less continuous, though the Platonism is much the same also in this area. Just as you have the Form of Equality for equating things, you have the Form of Goodness or Beauty to guide you in actions and designs. Just as equality is never experienced, so are Goodness and Beauty. You "grasp" the Forms, somewhat like you grasp that 1+1 = 2. You do not *see* that 1+1 = 2. You can see two apples next to each other and you can view them as individuals and add them up as "two apples." But then you are interpreting your experiences in an intelligent way. 1, 1, and 2 is not *all* the apples are, and they are not the *same* as 1, 1, and 2. Nor do you see a + between them, etc.[1]

Next let us see how Plato attempts to use dialectics to construct what is probably the most famous social utopia ever fashioned in the West: the Kallipolis.

---

[1] Platonism in metaphysics is the view that abstractions exist separately, that is independently from sensible or material particulars. For example, the Equal, as a Form, is something different from (roughly) equal sticks and stones. The sticks and stones come and go: nature forms them, and nature at some point takes them away. But the Equal stays forever, just as it is.
A main challenger to Platonism in metaphysics has been Aristotelianism. This is that abstractions exist *in* particulars somehow. The abstractions are real, the Aristotelian insists, and they are not simply the same as particulars, but the abstractions have no independent life of their own. A later alternative that emerged in the medieval period is "nominalism." This says that abstractions just do not exist. There are only particular, individual things — no kinds at all. All symbols that seem to be for kinds are just names: they do not describe anything that is really common to all the members of the kinds (beyond the name). For example, the word "cats" is just a label we put on all cats and only cats. But there is nothing that is specific or common to cats that makes them *deserve* this name. There is no set of core properties to unite the class, for example. It is just an accident that we do not have one dog in the class as well.
Jubien's book is an accessible introduction to metaphysics.

2.8 Utopia or Dystopia

First let us rehearse the big picture. Socrates' dialectics are ethical and skeptical, and Plato's are boldly metaphysical. From Plato we hear of some of the grandest thoughts ever produced by our species. When Socrates speaks we hear of criticism, criticism, and criticism. With Socrates we can never get very far up in the air, for doubts and problems will soon pull us back down to the earth. Socrates is the archetypal questioner. Plato, however, is the man with all the *answers* to the riddles of the universe, or so he seems to think. Both figures depend extensively on dialectic. Dialectic is the motor of their thought all along. But one is critical and one is bold.

In the *Republic* Plato advances a famous utopia. In some readers' eyes this has been a dystopia. We need now to consider whether Plato manages to build his utopia on a purely dialectical foundation. First we must understand some very basic features of Plato's utopianism, and then we can come to its basis, or its lack of basis, in dialectical reasoning.

The word "utopia" derives from the Greek *eu-topos*, which means no-place. Utopias are perfect societies that do not exist. But they are also societies that should or must exist. The word "dystopia" signifies a utopia that has gone wrong. It is a hell on earth, not a heaven on earth — so it is an antithesis. Plato's utopian thought can be interpreted in either way, as utopian or dystopian. The city he designs, named the Kallipolis, is either glorious or terrible, according to each interpreter who looks at it. Typically one does not find very moderate or indifferent views about it.

What is the Kallipolis like? And why should it be brought to existence? Its most basic feature is understood from this passage from an ancient Indian myth in the *Rig Veda*:

> The Purusa has a thousand heads, a thousand eyes, and a thousand feet. He, encompassing the world on all sides...
>
> The Purusa alone is all this universe, what has been, and what is to be.[1]
>
> When they divided the Purusa [...], into how many parts did they separate him? What did his mouth become? What his two arms? What are declared to be his two thighs, his two feet?
>
> The Brahman (priestly caste) was his mouth, his two arms became the Rajanya (warrior caste); his thighs are the Vaisya (artisan caste), from his two feet the Sudra (serf caste) was produced.[2]

---

[1] *Rig Veda* 10.90, 1–2; Edgerton p. 67.
[2] *Rig Veda* 10.90, 11–12; Edgerton p. 68.

The Purusa, which is the whole containing everything, divides naturally into specialized parts. The ancient Hindus believed that society needs to be hierarchical because individuals' natural abilities differ. Some are smart, so they should think. Some are courageous and strong, so they should be warriors. Some are handy, so they should work in the crafts. Some are not so good at anything and they should work like slaves, serving others without learning any special skills. (For what would happen otherwise? One would have cowards on the battle front, and terrible crafts, singers off key, etc.) This is the principle of *specialization* that is at work in ancient India and ancient Greece alike. What is its opposite? The principle that each individual should be self-sufficient. If you think for yourself and fight for yourself and make your own clothes, etc., then you are quite far away from specializing.

Specialization is something that Plato also believes in. But there is a notable difference between him and the Hinduists. This is that Plato is also a *meritocrat*. This means that in the Kallipolis there are strict tests for how well one performs in a professional position. If one shows talent then one advances, but if one fails to show talent, then one falls down the scale. It matters none at all whether one is female or male or what one's skin color is. It makes no difference if one's parents have or lack talent, because there is no assumption that the traits are inherited. In this way Plato's utopia is deeply rational. What it is not is traditional. One is not born into a *caste*, unlike in Hinduism. One can have talented parents and lack talents, or vice versa. These are facts that Plato would be the first to admit. He is an elitist, certainly, but he is not therefore a traditionalist or a conservative.

Plato's anti-traditionalism goes so far that he denies all rights to property. He is a *communist*. The idea is that citizens will work together only if they have belongings together. Otherwise they will look out for themselves, or for their families and friends, and then they will not work for the good of the entire whole. They will only use the city as a means. But they should view it as an end. That way, Plato says, the city has a good chance of becoming a good place! For whatever is used only as a means will hardly tend to reach perfection. It will be trampled down and abused if it fails to serve some ulterior end: that is what happens, after all, to slaves, to ageing machines, etc. If you want something to be respected then you need to have it be viewed as an end, not as a means. Then it is something for which you sacrifice things and not something you sacrifice for other things.

But Plato's anti-traditionalism goes further than this. He also wants to break apart the *family* unit because it holds back the development of the city and of the individuals in it. Parents will be too biased to look at their children for what they are. Consequently, they hold their children back from flourishing according to their real natures. The generalization for Plato is that if you drop away private property and the family unit then there will be fewer biases and, at the same time, a much more realistic basis for the development of individuals and groups alike.

In sum, Plato's utopia is *specialized*, *communistic*, and *polygamistic*. This is heaven or hell, utopia or dystopia, depending where you happen to be standing.

Later in history many utopias have the features of Plato's Kallipolis because they follow Plato more or less consciously. Communism is a very widespread ideal in them, and so is polygamy (or celibacy, as among the Rappites and the Shakers). One may compare the diverse utopias of the Renaissance and of the Industrial era, and this is what one often finds.[1] Utopias are often built for the sake of social unity, and communism and polygamy are for good reason taken for deep aspects of this. Why? Because it tends to be property and the family that we value. We work and we love. These are the great concerns of human life everywhere. Plato reasons well when he makes property and family life so relevant to politics.

The idea of specialization demands our closer attention. It is less popular in the history of utopias, but it is in a way the very core of Plato's own utopia. In the Kallipolis there are three social classes, the rational, the emotional, and the physical. All of these are needed for the whole. The rational class rules over the whole and the emotional and the physical have their places. The picture is in major respects like in the *Rig Veda*.

Why does any rational class have to come along to rule everyone? Why does Plato believe that specialization cannot be set up in a democracy? He answers this in the *Republic*:

> Yes, I said, [*the democratic man*] lives from day to day indulging the appetite of the hour; and sometimes he is lapped in drink and strains of the flute; then he becomes a water-drinker, and tries to get thin; then he takes a turn at gymnastics; sometimes idling and neglecting everything, then once more living the life of a philosopher; often he is busy with politics, and starts to his feet and says and does whatever comes into his head; and, if he is emulous of anyone who is a warrior, off he is in that direction, or of men of business, once more in that.

---

[1] On the history of utopian designs see Manuel and Manuel.

His life has neither law nor order; and this distracted existence he terms joy and bliss and freedom; and so he goes on.

Yes, he replied, he is all liberty and equality.[1]

If we have many different impulses and aims and no guiding principles then we will not know a proper time and place for each of our several aims and activities. There will be no grand plan to steer us. And hence we will end up contradicting ourselves. We will feast on one day and diet on the next, rush to philosophy or politics and rush back out without having understood anything, etc. That is why there must be an elite, Plato says:

> Come then, I said, and as the general umpire in theatrical contests proclaims the result, do you also decide who in your opinion is first in the scale of happiness, and who second, and in what order the others follow: there are five of them in all—they are the royal, timocratical, oligarchical, democratical, tyrannical. [...] Need we hire a herald, or shall I announce, that the son of Ariston *[the best]* has decided that the best and justest is also the happiest, and that this is he who is the most royal man and king over himself; and that the worst and most unjust man is also the most miserable, and that this is he who being the greatest tyrant of himself is also the greatest tyrant of his State?
>
> Make the proclamation yourself, he said.
>
> And shall I add, "whether seen or unseen by gods and men"?
>
> Let the words be added.[2]

Plato is an aristocrat. He believes that an elite should rule in a *polis* (city) as well as a *psyche* (soul). Just as the perfect city is hierarchical, so is the ideal soul. Both demand planning and co-ordination because both are complex.[3]

Now we can turn to dialectics.

What does the Kallipolis have to do with dialectics? Well, what the rational elite's authority is ultimately founded on for Plato is their knowledge of the self-predicated Forms or Ideas, and they reach this end by means of dialectic. In other words, the self-relational patterns are the real authorities. They are the models or blueprints or archetypes that the rational leaders must look to, or they are not qualified to rule. The Forms are perfect, like human beings never are. Even the elite,

---

1 561C–E.
2 580B–C.
3 There is much in the *Republic* that I am skipping over. One such thing is this *psyche–polis* analogy. Some scholars argue that Plato's purpose in the *Republic* is to present an ideal of a perfect *psyche* and not of a perfect *polis*. Probably the more realistic story is that he is after both (compare the *Laws* for Plato's hierarchical views in politics).

being only human, is ape-like in comparison to these rational objects of perfection. What is more, there is a Form *of* Forms in the Republic, the Form of the Good. The Good stands to the other Forms like the other Forms stand to all things that are not Forms. So the Good is at the top of the whole pyramid. You cannot get higher than that.

Well, what *is* the Good? What does Plato say? The irony is that he does not know. He offers only metaphors and mythical descriptions of it because so far he has attained nothing better. (He would prefer to offer crisp definitions, but he is unable to provide them, he says. He is not yet advanced enough.) Here is one of the metaphorical descriptions. It compares thought with vision (and here Plato's fictional "Socrates" leads the way while Glaucon tries to understand):

But you see that without the addition of some other nature there is no seeing or being seen?

How do you mean?

Sight being, as I conceive, in the eyes, and he who has eyes wanting to see; colour being also present in them, still unless there be a third nature specially adapted to the purpose, the owner of the eyes will see nothing and the colours will be invisible.

Of what nature are you speaking?

Of that which you term light, I replied.

True, he said.

Noble, then, is the bond which links together sight and visibility, and great beyond other bonds by no small difference of nature; for light is their bond, and light is no ignoble thing?

Nay, he said, the reverse of ignoble.

And which, I said, of the gods in heaven would you say was the lord of this element? Whose is that light which makes the eye to see perfectly and the visible to appear?

You mean the sun, as you and all mankind say.

May not the relation of sight to this deity be described as follows?

How?

Neither sight nor the eye in which sight resides is the sun?

No.

Yet of all the organs of sense the eye is the most like the sun?

By far the most like.

And the power which the eye possesses is a sort of effluence which is dispensed from the sun?

Exactly.

Then the sun is not sight, but the author of sight who is recognized by sight?

True, he said.

And this is he whom I call the child of the good, whom the good begat in his own likeness, to be in the visible world, in relation to sight and the things of sight, what the good is in the intellectual world in relation to mind and the things of mind.

Will you be a little more explicit? he said.

Why, you know, I said, that the eyes, when a person directs them towards objects on which the light of day is no longer shining, but the moon and stars only, see dimly, and are nearly blind; they seem to have no clearness of vision in them?

Very true.

But when they are directed towards objects on which the sun shines, they see clearly and there is sight in them?

Certainly.

And the soul is like the eye: when resting upon that on which truth and being shine, the soul perceives and understands, and is radiant with intelligence; but when turned towards the twilight of becoming and perishing, then she has opinion only, and goes blinking about, and is first of one opinion and then of another, and seems to have no intelligence?

Just so.

Now, that which imparts truth to the known and the power of knowing to the knower is what I would have you term the idea of good, and this you will deem to be the cause of science, and of truth in so far as the latter becomes the subject of knowledge; beautiful too, as are both truth and knowledge, you will be right in esteeming this other nature as more beautiful than either; and, as in the previous instance, light and sight may be truly said to be like the sun, and yet not to be the sun, so in this other sphere, science and truth may be deemed to be like the good, but not the good; the good has a place of honour yet higher.[1]

Sight is nothing without light, and light comes from the sun. The sun illuminates things for us to see. But most of all it illuminates itself, as it is itself the brightest thing by far. In this way the sun seems roughly to be self-predicated. Now, we are to notice an *analogy* between the sun and the Good. Thought depends on the "light" that shines down from the Good. The Good "illuminates" things, making them intelligible, not visible. But the Good also illuminates *itself*, and this it illuminates more than anything else, so it is the most intelligible thing there is. In

---

[1] 507D–509A.

different terms, the sun and the Good are similar to each other in that they provide such a fundamental service to everyone while at the same time serving themselves most of all.

Plato's self-relational ideal should be at least vaguely familiar from the dialectics that we have met with in this book already. Here are the basic associations (with Plato's fictional "Socrates" teaching Glaucon again):

> Until the person is able to abstract and define rationally the idea of good, and unless he can run the gauntlet of all objections, and is ready to disprove them, not by appeals to opinion, but to absolute truth, never faltering at any step of the argument—unless he can do all this, you would say that he knows neither the idea of good nor any other good; he apprehends only a shadow, if anything at all, which is given by opinion and not by science;—dreaming and slumbering in this life, before he is well awake here, he arrives at the world below, and has his final quietus.

> In all that I should most certainly agree with you.

> And surely you would not have the children of your ideal State, whom you are nurturing and educating—if the ideal ever becomes a reality—you would not allow the future rulers to be like posts (Literally 'lines,' probably the starting-point of a race-course.), having no reason in them, and yet to be set in authority over the highest matters?

> Certainly not.

> Then you will make a law that they shall have such an education as will enable them to attain the greatest skill in asking and answering questions?

> Yes, he said, you and I together will make it.

> Dialectic, then, as you will agree, is the coping-stone of the sciences, and is set over them; no other science can be placed higher—the nature of knowledge can no further go?

> I agree, he said.[1]

The Good makes its appearance to the rulers because they practice *dialectics*. They ask and answer questions until the very end. They keep asking *why* something should be until further asking proves to be impossible, and they will ask *what* something is until it is equally certain. The only way they can possibly stop, if they are fully rational or careful enough to qualify as dialecticians in an exact sense, Plato says, is by ending up with a hierarchy of Forms. Why is that? The dialectical answers we have surveyed have all been self-relational. Series of

---

[1] 534B–535A.

questions have terminated in self-relations every time. But the Good *is* a self-relation, so it is just the familiar kind of termination point. The dialectical patterns we are dealing with are continually the same. The *Republic* repeats the same patterns that we have been using all along.[1]

Now, does Plato manage to construct his Kallipolis purely on a dialectical foundation? This is the critical question. We need to view it from both sides.

Let us first look at the negative answer that can be given. The reason why Plato does not succeed in basing his utopia on dialectics is that, on one level, dialectics is not political at all. For Plato's utopian elite cannot possibly only philosophize about absolutes if it is to be a *political* elite. It must also *rule*. There have to be practical applications of the high-minded philosophical principles or the elite's education is politically irrelevant. Hence, if the elite's dialectics will have taken them to the Good at some point then after this highpoint has been reached the elite's members will need to come back down to the mundane *polis* to use their knowledge. The educated leaders must come down to the city to shape this city into a utopia. Therefore their knowledge should not be pure knowledge but "know-how" of some sort. It needs to be useful knowledge. So the utopian leaders must, as it were, keep their eyes fixed on the Good, or maintain it alive in their memories, while manipulating the city to match it as closely as possible.

Plato sees this difficulty clearly. He tries to avoid it by portraying two directions for dialectics, the *ascending* and the *descending*. As a philosopher one "rises" to the Forms, and ultimately to the Good. That is at the same time to rise from the material concerns that predominate in the ordinary, pre-utopian, *polis* and in the lower tiers of the psyche. But once one has reached the top of the ascent, by grasping the Good, one needs to go back down. The ascent consists of something that we already studied, namely questions and answers. This is the familiar dialectical procedure in which one aims at the fundamental or absolute limit or self-relation. The aim is to come to the highest principles. The descending dialectic, however, consists only of the *application* of the principles. Now one does not ask or inquire. Now one takes what one has learned *already*, as a philosopher, and puts it to practice. Now one does not ask but commands, or obeys the commands that were made from the heights.

This is a sketch of the total procedure that Plato outlines in the *Republic*. It may be pictured as an ascent up to the top of a mountain and

---

[1] This is only approximately true. The *hierarchy* of Forms is not found in Socrates' dialectics, for example. For more on the *Republic* see Reeve.

then as a descent back down to the plains that surround the mountain. At the mountain's top you find perfect knowledge but the city is in the valley below, so you must go back down or your knowledge is of no political use.

Now, what is wrong with this position of Plato's is that the descending dialectic Plato envisions in the *Republic* is no dialectic at all. If it were then an activity as dull as the counting of a chain's middle links *after* one has explored the chain's ends would be considered something critical or free or self-relational. But it is not. For if one works with applications and no longer with principles then one has lost one's freedom. If one only obeys principles that have been laid down in advance then one operates like a slave! In a similar vein, the critical spirit is then gone. If one does not get to ask or to explore anymore, and if one has only to get to work, then there is no talk anymore about pushing the limits or opening new horizons. Plato's "descents" are something demeaning. They are not *dialectics*. They are not inquiries into absolutes.

But Plato has thought of this as well. In a sense he admits that there is something artificial in linking philosophers with politics, for he says:

> [...] neither the uneducated and uninformed of the truth, nor yet those who never make an end of their education, will be able ministers of State; not the former, because they have no single aim of duty which is the rule of all their actions, private as well as public; nor the latter, because they will not act at all except upon compulsion, fancying that they are already dwelling apart in the islands of the blest.
>
> Very true, he replied.
>
> Then, I said, the business of us who are the founders of the State will be to compel the best minds to attain that knowledge which we have already shown to be the greatest of all—they must continue to ascend until they arrive at the good; but when they have ascended and seen enough we must not allow them to do as they do now.
>
> What do you mean?
>
> I mean that they remain in the upper world: but this must not be allowed; they must be made to descend again among the prisoners in the den, and partake of their labors and honors, whether they are worth having or not.
>
> But is not this unjust? he said; ought we to give them a worse life, when they might have a better?
>
> You have again forgotten, my friend, I said, the intention of the legislator, who did not aim at making any one class in the State happy above the rest; the happiness was to be in the whole State, and he

held the citizens together by persuasion and necessity, making them benefactors of the State, and therefore benefactors of one another; to this end he created them, not to please themselves, but to be his instruments in binding up the State.[1]

Inherently the philosophers have a drive only to ascend, and once they have reached the culmination point of their dialectics their wish is to stay in that upper region of things. In other words, there is nothing philosophical or dialectical about coming back down. There is nothing free about it either, for the descent must be forced — as Plato has just said in the preceding excerpt. Nonetheless, Plato does, admittedly, give a reason why the philosophers should be forced to descend: this will, he says, be better for the whole of the *polis*. The philosophers should think of the advantage of the entire *polis* and not only of the advantage of the philosophers. But notice that this is not the *philosophers'* angle. As dialecticians they have *not* come to value the whole polis above other things. (The overwhelming value of the whole is defended by "Socrates," that is Plato's mouthpiece in this dialogue. But this "Socrates" is not a philosopher proper. Why not? He does not ascend to the Forms and the Good. He offers, as he says, mere myths or allegories where a proper dialectician would give a self-evident answer to a series of critical questions. "Socrates" in this dialogue is just some man in the street, not a proper dialectician!)

Now we have seen why Plato's utopianism seems to lack a dialectical foundation. Next let us view the same matter backwards. What in dialectics speaks *for* Plato's utopianism?

We need first to notice in what sense Socrates' message in 2.1 and 2.2 was political. He said that specialists mistake themselves for more than specialists. They normally believe that they have generalizable knowledge. But the fact is that this is always only a case of having a hammer and seeing nails. It indicates a lack of imagination, not an ability to issue proofs. For Socrates, it is normal not to know how little one knows. His world is rife with little imperialists. Now, this is a political message because it is a generalization about individuals' relations in society. It implies that there should be limits to what specialists can decide. In this way Socrates' social ethos is broadly anti-totalitarian. Socrates is not apolitical.

But this is not the whole of Socrates' social message. He does not hold that there are no real authorities. Nor does he favor the majority vote. He obviously rebels against the majority's view in the *Apology*, as we saw. He is for the authority of *dialectics*. If you will, he is not

---

[1] 519B–520A.

a democrat or an aristocrat but a "dialectocrat." But in this sense he agrees with Plato's utopianism! Dialectic is the social authority both believe in.

Does this mean that Socrates would want to be a dictator of Athens? In a way it seems so, given that Socrates believes himself to be the wisest. His self-image is that of a teacher of the public. But he also seeks to learn from others, and he is self-ironic, so he is hardly positioned, in his own view, to issue commands to others, or to preach his lessons. What he is qualified to do, in his own view, is to pose his characteristic questions. Also recall that he believes in questioning everyone, young and old, rich and poor. In this way he actually attempts to get everyone to do dialectics. He says that the examined life is something for everyone. Hence, in conclusion of our discussion of the Kallipolis we may say that Socrates would agree with Plato that there must be a dictatorship of the dialecticians but he would disagree with Plato that there needs therefore to be a social elite.

Now we are almost done with our discussion of the dialectics of Socrates and Plato. What remains is Plato's theology.

2.9 God

Plato's *Laws* contains this famous argument for the existence of God:

[Athenian Stranger] Let us assume that there is a motion able to move other things, but not to move itself;—that is one kind; and there is another kind which can move itself as well as other things, working in composition and decomposition, by increase and diminution and generation and destruction—that is also one of the many kinds of motion.[1] [...]

[Cleinias] What do you mean?

[Ath.] I mean this: when one thing changes another, and that another, of such will there be any primary changing element? How can a thing which is moved by another ever be the beginning of change? Impossible. But when the self-moved changes other, and that again other, and thus thousands upon tens of thousands of bodies are set in motion, must not the beginning of all this motion be the change of the self-moving principle?

[Cle.] Very true, and I quite agree.

[Ath.] Or, to put the question in another way, making answer to ourselves:—If, as most of these philosophers have the audacity to affirm, all things were at rest in one mass, which of the above-mentioned principles of motion would first spring up among them?

---

[1] 894B–C.

[Cle.] Clearly the self-moving; for there could be no change in them arising out of any external cause; the change must first take place in themselves.

[Ath.] Then we must say that self-motion being the origin of all motions, and the first which arises among things at rest as well as among things in motion, is the eldest and mightiest principle of change, and that which is changed by another and yet moves other is second.

[Cle.] Quite true.[1]

This is an early version of what is later called the "cosmological argument" or the "cosmological proof," which will be a major topic in the next chapter on Kant. It states that the most radical movers must have come *first* in time. The beginning of motion must have been in self-motion, and this must have caused the less dramatic kinds of movement. Why did self-motion have to come first? For the dialectical reasons that are familiar by now. A series of movements cannot *begin* from external causes, any more than a puppet on a string can *begin* a series of movements. There cannot be strings attached to the *first* mover. Otherwise it just would not be the *first!* If the puppeteer moves first then we need her to be autonomous. If she is controlled by the playwright then we can hope that the *playwright* is the prime mover. But *whoever* is first must be self-moved. We cannot possibly ever arrive at a first link in the series of movements that is not a self-mover. So the only sensible beginning is independent.[2] Nothing else *makes sense.* Here we have a typical "rationalist" argument. It is not an effort to accord with experience. It is an effort to compel by reasoning.

By the time of the *Laws* Plato has moved beyond not only Socrates but also the Forms and Ideas. But has he moved beyond dialectics? No. For the above reasoning is plainly dialectical. As before, Plato works

---

[1] 894E–895B.
[2] I am simplifying again. The *Laws* actually contains a hierarchy of *ten*, not two, types of motion. There are several *gradations* between the extremes. Roughly, rolling or spinning around an axis is closer to self-motion than is a movement of revolving around an external body. But self-motion is extensionless and precise. Rolling or spinning already involves a distinction between a center and a periphery, and revolving around a separate center is even less centered. Yet self-motion is at the top of the hierarchy, being most focused.
The formal pattern aRbRc...zRz (or zRR) is actually *blind* to this hierarchy. For in the formal pattern R only repeats. It does not get more intense or superlative. This is a drawback in the formal expression. (If one wrote a‹b‹c...z‹z (or ...z‹‹) then this would not remedy the situation, because then ‹ would repeat.) Here is one point at which one may attempt to improve on this book's theory of dialectic.

with the form aRbRcRd...zRz (or ...zRR, depending on how we read him exactly).

Is this theological dialectic valid? One thing that Kant will question about it in the next chapter is our certainty that there ever *was* a first mover. If there was a first mover then Plato may be right. But was there? That is one issue to raise.

A different question would be whether Plato's theology coheres at all with modern science. He represents what is in a way the opposite of another theorist of origins, Darwin. For in the *Origin of Species* Darwin locates the more autonomous organisms at a *later* stage in natural history. First come germs, fishes, etc., that is highly *dependent* movers. Animals like turtles and sharks are more capable of originating their own motions, and they come *later* in history. But there is also a sense in which Darwin does not contradict Plato at all, because in Darwin's world *no one* is a self-mover. All organisms adapt to their environments in Darwin. Purposes like adaption, survival, and reproduction, dominate all organisms in Darwin's natural world. There is a dictatorship of the environment! No one has creative autonomy or the full freedom to reason. Nature sets everyone's agenda. Hence there *are no* first movers in Darwin. Darwin's theory of evolution is in fact not intended at all as an answer to the question of ultimate origins. Due to that reason Darwin's theory is not a competitor to Plato's. It just does not aim for the same position. So it is not really an opposite at all, contrary to first impressions.

Well, how about the Big Bang? Instead of confronting the complex facts of modern physics we do better to tackle this topic by means of the dialectics of Kant.

Further Reading

M. G. J. Beets: *Socrates on Death and the Beyond.* This is an old personal favorite of mine that may be hard to find for some readers.

Werner Jaeger: *Paideia*, 3 Volumes. This trilogy is rich on the cultural context of Plato's work, philosophical and otherwise.

Michael Jubien: *Contemporary Metaphysics: An Introduction.* This is an easy to read and its perspectives are varied and stimulating.

Plato: *Dialogues.* There is nothing like reading the originals. The older translations are available cost-free online.

A.E. Taylor: *Plato: The Man and His Work.* This book is accessible as well as detailed. Many current scholars would say it is outdated, but it manages to discuss deep philosophical questions without losing in precision or rigor. It, too, is available cost-free online.

Gregory Vlastos: *Socrates.* Here is another accessible work, from one of the most influential recent scholars of ancient Greek philosophy. This is a highly readable book but it makes Socrates' thought quite moderate. It cannot explain what Socrates dies for.

(See the Bibliography at the end of this book for detailed information on these and other titles.)

CHAPTER 3. KANT

Sapere aude! (Latin for: *Dare to think!, or Dare to know!*)
— Kant

When we approach Immanuel Kant, we leap over two millennia. We leave behind Hellenic Greece with its diverse philosophies and scientific discoveries, Rome with its empire, the slow Medieval period, the flourishing Renaissance, and the ages of philosophical Rationalism and Empiricism in the seventeenth and eighteenth centuries. After all this has happened, Kant comes along to make a "Copernican Revolution" in philosophy.

What does Kant say? His philosophy divides into two large halves. The first half merges reasoning with experience, and this has little to do with dialectics so I will not go into it. The second half is dialectical, and it is about transforming reasoning from a cosmological force of nature into an ethical plan of action.[1] Kant's great point about dialectics is that they do not measure the world as it *is*. What dialectics do is tell us what to think and *do*. They are rules about what *should* exist, not what *does* exist. In this they are more like the laws of legal codes than the laws of physics: they are rules *to be* abided by, not laws *already* abided by. This is what Kant teaches. But one should not make the mistake of thinking that Kant holds some particular country to have the right legal code already. That Kant would

---

[1] These halves correspond to the first and second halves of the *Critique of Pure Reason*. Kant's second *Critique*, on practical reason, elaborates on the second half. The third and last *Critique*, on art and the beauty of nature, tries to reconcile the two halves.
For introductions to Kant, see Beiser and Allison.

never say. Perfect countries do not exist. The most perfect laws exist only in our minds. We can dig them up if we think clearly and exhibit enough courage. We must dare to think, as Kant says: *Sapere aude!* This is the only pathway to the Kingdom of Ends, as he calls it. No country's laws or conventions will be reliable by comparison.

I will begin this chapter with Kant's "antinomies." Then I introduce his ethical and anti-metaphysical turn. Next I expose the dialectics of choice, autonomy, and heteronomy. This brings me conveniently to Kant's "paralogisms" and finally to Kant's view of Plato.

3.1 The Antinomies

Kant presents four antinomies, and each of the antinomies consists of a thesis and an antithesis which opposes the thesis. So there are four different conflicts. Here is the first:

Thesis 1:
> Reality has a beginning in space and time.

Antithesis 1:
> Reality has no beginning, so reality extends without limit in space as well as time.

This is the second:
Thesis 2:
> There are, besides complex things *made* of individuals, partless and indivisible individuals. I.e., there are simple things somewhere.

Antithesis 2:
> There are no individuals but only complexes, all the way down. Every part will have parts, and likewise every whole will belong to an even greater whole. There are no limits at either end.

The third:
Thesis 3:
> There are beginnings to causal chains. There are first links, not only second links, third links, etc.

Antithesis 3:
> Every event has a prior cause, so there are no beginnings. There is only a continuous stream.

The fourth:
Thesis 4:
> Something in reality must be unconditioned, i.e., necessary, absolutely. It may be a part of reality or all of reality, but everything cannot be only conditioned, possible, or accidental.

Antithesis 4:

Reality is conditioned all the way through, so everything is contingent. Nothing absolute or necessary exists, and everything depends on something further for its character and its existence.

Thesis 1 and antithesis 1 oppose each other, and so do thesis 2 and antithesis 2, etc. So there are four pairs, and the members of the pairs try to rule each other out.

Now let us look at the pairs of theses and antitheses taken individually not only as statements but as arguments with reasons to back up the statements. Here is the first pair:

Thesis 1:

One must be able, at some point in history, to complete the list of events in time and space that makes up the whole of history.

It is unimaginable that the whole list of events cannot be surveyed. In other words, there must be a greatest whole to which everything belongs. The whole may be greater than some region, to be sure, so it may need extending somewhere. But it cannot *always* need extending. There must be a list *somewhere* that is complete. Perhaps humans cannot reach it, but it must be there to reach ayway. It must be possible to draw, from somewhere, at some time.

Antithesis 1:

If there are limits somewhere then the question is begged what lies beyond them. But what lies beyond them cannot be nothing, for empty time and empty space are unimaginable.

If there was a time during which nothing seemed to occur we nonetheless imagine that that period was perfectly valid as a period of time. Then we inquire what happened in that period. We cannot leave the matter blank. But likewise with space. We cannot just close the book. Beyond each limit there must be *something*.

The reasons here given on both sides of the contest add depth to that contest. They do not make the conflict any easier. On the contrary: the gap only grows. One can feel the pull of *both* sides, not only of one side or the other. This same thing happens with every one of the pairs.

Here is the second pair of reasons, to support the second thesis and antithesis, respectively:

Thesis 2:

It would be impossible to think about anything in a complete way if each thing had an infinitude of parts. One could never list all of the parts.

Similarly, the largest whole could not possibly be completed unless there are real limits to things. One would always be in a corner of the universe only, not in the widest open place.

We cannot *think* of things without considering them as having limits. Thinking beings cannot get along only with incomplete objects.

Antithesis 2:

Empirically we find smaller and smaller parts and greater and greater wholes, as our microscopes and telescopes improve.

Hence, what we have *evidence* for, always, is just a further continuation of part-whole relations, in both directions, the smaller and the larger. This will not change unless we stop researching. But stopping research would only indicate a choice of ours, and it would not show anything about how things really are. If we look at how things really are then we will keep on finding ever-smaller parts and always-larger wholes.

The third pair of reasons is this:

Thesis 3:

If you give the cause of an event then that cause is the *whole* cause. In other words, if there is to be accountability, if anyone is ever going to be able to say or think that x causes y, then x must be a spontaneous mover.

Consider what would happen otherwise. If x is caused, in turn, by v, then x by itself did *not* cause y. Then invoking x would *not* explain the occurrence of y. Would v? Well, only if it had no prior cause u, etc. At *some* point there must be self-causation or there are no explanations but only endless streams without definite characteristics.

Antithesis 3:

We do not understand spontaneous leaps, so if there are godly creations or freely willed acts then the only way we can explain them is by looking at what formed them. But that is exactly to *deny* that they had no prior causes. *So* we have to deny the prior causes.

In other words, if we place a limit somewhere then it will be necessary to inquire what is beyond the limit. This is so in causal thinking just as it is so regarding the limits of space and time and parts and wholes. (The same pattern recurs in human thought, paradox in and paradox out.)

Here is the fourth and final pair:

Thesis 4:

Things are explained by saying, or thinking, why they *have to* be or exist. There are no authoritative accounts which report only arbitrary numbers and wild guesses. The only way to think with any firmness is by finding the deeper structures of things.

Given this, if one is confronted with something that seems accidental and contingent then one needs to search underneath the surface to find something harder and less shaky to base it on. Otherwise one will be only throwing colors in the wind. There must be something, at least *one* thing, that could not be otherwise. There must be something original that *had to* come. That may then be built on to explain the rest of what happens.

Put differently, if a thing hangs from another thing then that other thing cannot always just hang from something further. Something must be there on its own. The whole edifice cannot float in the air.

Antithesis 4:

As a matter of fact we do not find anything necessary in the world, but always only accidents after accidents. Everything could be different. This is a world of conditions without end, whether one is comfortable with this or not.

Moreover, the fact is that *thoughts* about causes are not causes. If we study the world empirically then what we find is often different from what we thought we would find. Arguments about God are about our beliefs, not about the world as we find it. We may in fact find quite a mess of things if we inquire, and this may be an enormously complex universe! It may not be very orderly, but it is what there is. It matters comparatively little what we would like to find or even what we insist on finding. Such feelings reveal things about us, not about reality.

(I should note at this point that these are *my* wordings of Kant's antinomies. I do not follow Kant to the letter. I try to explain him, and I would not do that by simply quoting him. Moreover, my hope here is to introduce the reader to Kant's complex philosophy. My versions should be more accessible to the reader than Kant's original formulations are, so that the reader can find a point of entry to Kant's maze. Let no one think that Kant's thought-world is not a maze, however! It is truly complex. What the reader has just read is my simplification, not Kant himself.)

So now we have antinomies, and there are gaps between ways of reasoning. Now what?

Here is what Kant says. Each of these pieces of reasoning makes good sense. There is a first in each series or not. If there is not then there is an endless series. There will be a final point or there will never be one. It is either/or. Both alternatives make sense, so there is a paradox — or an "antinomy," as Kant calls it.

It is important to notice that each of the theses and antitheses can seem to make compelling sense if it is considered *separately*, that is without its opponent. If one were unimaginative, or if one grew up in a backward place, then one might simply go along with one or the other of each pair of arguments and be satisfied that one is rational. But the true story is that every argument has an alternative, a competitor. Every argument has an enemy! And the enemy is just as good, just as valid. That is what leads to the problems.

What conclusion does Kant draw from this? He says that *no one* is right about these extreme questions. This is striking. It is a surprising lesson to draw from the antinomies because the antinomies seem to confront us with a choice. The antinomies seem to tell us that from each pair of arguments we should choose one or the other. But Kant actually tells us to deny *both* alternatives in every pair. (Metaphorically, Kant is like a parent who refuses to take the side of either of his bickering children.)

This is the lesson Kant draws, but it is not the kind of lesson that everyone might be as inclined to draw. For example, an anthropologist who meets with many different cultures across the globe might conclude differently if she came across a similar plethora of arguments on her travels. She might say, as a relativist, that each of the arguments is good as it is. She could try to manage this by *localizing* them. In one quarter of the world thesis 1 would be true and in another it would be false, and in this latter place the antithesis would be true instead; and likewise for 2, 3, and 4. This way the anthropologist would localize metaphysical beliefs. One could be right in Papua New Guinea in exactly the same way that one is *wrong* in India. But this is not what Kant says. He does not accept any doctrine of local knowledge, or any generalization, which would be similar in principle, that one individual can be right *for* that individual. No, for Kant there is only one real world, and everyone has to be right or wrong in exactly the same way. No truths are local. Everyone is *not* right about these fundamental issues. Everyone is *wrong* about them.

How can *all* the theses and antitheses be wrong? Kant calls dialectic "the logic of illusion."[1] All humans are prone to the same illusions because the dialectical patterns are internal to us all. Humans, or reasoning beings in general, are always capable of feeling *both* that space must have an end *and* that it cannot. Similarly, time must and cannot begin; chains of causes must but also cannot begin somewhere; and the smallest parts and the greatest wholes have to but also cannot exist. Whatever we may happen to hear of first does not matter. If we hear about all the theses and all the antitheses then the result is that we will feel the pull in *every* direction. So if you took someone from Papua New Guinea and transported her to India, at a sufficiently receptive age, then you would get her to feel the tensions of Kant's antinomies (assuming,

---

[1] *Critique of Pure Reason* A292/B348.

that is, that in these two places some pair of thesis and antithesis predominates). Kant holds that the antinomies are everyone's illusions. Every individual can in principle be brought to suffer from them. For these are simply the capabilities of the human mind.

But what Kant is really saying by means of all this is that these extreme issues are simply *beyond our capabilities* even though we find them so fascinating. Every new human generation seems to confront the same dilemmas. The unsettling implication is that we are bound always to have more questions than answers. Our intellectual curiosity extends our actual ability to reason! So there is something wrong with our thinking, and we are not really entitled to trust our own thoughts. We will never know whether God exists, whether there really is such a thing as free will, where we came from, where we will end up, etc. All the big questions of life are beyond us! This is what Kant is implying.

In different terms, Kant is saying that it is *dialectic* that gets us into trouble. It is as *dialecticians* that we think too big. Is he correct in this verdict? Is dialectic the logic of illusion?

Not exactly, for there is firm evidence that the antinomies contain only a *part* of dialectics. Dialectics can, on the one hand, be formulated as series like aRbRc..., as in the preceding chapters of this book. But on the other hand it is equally clear that self-relations are missing from the antinomies, so we need to say that Kant's dialectics are dialectics only to an extent. They are half-dialectics, having only one of the two formal pieces we outlined in the Introduction to this book.

We can easily isolate these two formal pieces. On the one hand, the antinomies' theses and antitheses can always be formulated as chains, like this:

formally: aRbRc...
antinomy 1: a precedes b precedes c...
antinomy 2: a is a part of b is a part of c...
antinomy 3: a causes b causes c...
antinomy 4: a necessitates b necessitates c...[1]

But on the other hand the antinomies never contain any of *these* patterns:

aRa...
RRa...
...zRz.
...zRR.

---

[1] I am simplifying. Actually, no antinomy consists of a series, as each antinomy consists of a pair of two competing series. In each pair one series ends and the other does not.

That is, Kant's antinomies involve no self-relations. *If* they did *then* he could say that it is *dialectic* that deserves the blame for the illusions of the antinomies. But as it is dialectic is innocent, and Kant is himself guilty of overlooking self-relations. For it is the self-relations that answer dialectical questions according to dialecticians, as we noted already in the Introduction. Hinduists as well as Platonists and Hegelians maintain that the limits are in selves. They do not maintain that there are spontaneous beginnings without selves, e.g. in sudden, arbitrary, reasonless leaps. We will come back to this error in Kant at the end of this chapter.

Now we need to come to understand how there is a brighter side to Kant's philosophy. This comes into view once we begin to see how reasoning is rich in creative powers. The antinomies actually testify to this. They are dead ends of reasoning, yes, but they do not really arise because we *lack* answers to the big questions. For in a way the antinomies are generated precisely because there are *too many* answers and reasons! There is one for each thesis *and* also one for its opposite or antithesis. We are capable of reasoning in too *many* consistent ways, not in too few. We are too inventive to solve the riddles of the universe in any one way. We are capable of making up and understanding many different lines of thought. We are not tied down by our senses, or by local cultures. Our thoughts can fly much more independently than empiricists or cultural relativists would have it. This can actually sound rather nice. And this is something Kant also means to say. He *does* think highly of human powers of reasoning. He *is* the man to say *Sapere aude!*, despite the antinomies. We *are* to reason, he says, only in a different way. What way?

3.2 Regulative Reasoning

The core of Kant's great turn regarding reasoning is this:

> In neither case—the regressus in infinitum, nor the regressus in indefinitum, is the series of conditions to be considered as actually infinite in the object itself. This might be true of things in themselves, but it cannot be asserted of phenomena, which, as conditions of each other, are only given in the empirical regress itself. Hence, the question no longer is, "What is the quantity of this series of conditions in itself—is it finite or infinite?" for it is nothing in itself; but, "How is the empirical regress to be commenced, and how far ought we to proceed with it?"[1]

---

[1] *Critique of Pure Reason* A512/B540.

There is no answer to the question whether the grandiose series that we happen to be considering in whichever antinomy *is* finite or infinite. What there is an answer to is how far we *ought* to go. What should we do? Where should we stop? Reasoning is for Kant something which gives us answers about what we do best to think and will and do. It is all about ideals. Nothing outside our reasoning needs to correspond with our reasoning. We need no external justification. If there is no God to accord with our thoughts then that does not count against our thoughts, Kant says. We do not *need* any independent justification. Hence it is not so bad that we do not have it either.

This is where we come face to face with the Kant who says *Sapere aude!* Kant applauds and endorses and enhances our abilities to reason so that we may *live* better, not that we should *know* about reality.

This implies, for Kant, that we need to adapt to a kind of dualism. We are to reason about values and not to reason about facts. The facts of reality demand from us something other than reasoning, namely observation and experiment. So there are, as it were, two different dimensions or levels to things in Kant. We need reason for ethics but we need observation for reality, and we need to keep these halves clearly apart from each other. Consider the realistic half first:

> Man is himself a phenomenon. His will has an empirical character, which is the empirical cause of all his actions. There is no condition—determining man and his volition in conformity with this character—which does not itself form part of the series of effects in nature, and is subject to their law—the law according to which an empirically undetermined cause of an event in time cannot exist. For this reason no given action can have an absolute and spontaneous origination, all actions being phenomena, and belonging to the world of experience.[1]

Experience teaches that this is how things work. Even humans are, for empirical science, basically animals. We may be intelligent as animals but we are thoroughly mechanical, according to science. But then there is this other side to things:

> But it cannot be said of reason, that the state in which it determines the will is always preceded by some other state determining it. For reason is not a phenomenon, and therefore not subject to sensuous conditions; and, consequently, even in relation to its causality, the sequence or conditions of time do not influence reason, nor can the dynamical law of nature, which determines the sequence of time according to certain rules, be applied to it. Reason is consequently the permanent condition of all actions of the human will. Each of

---

[1] *Critique of Pure Reason* A549/B577.

these is determined in the empirical character of the man, even before it has taken place. The intelligible character, of which the former is but the sensuous schema, knows no before or after; and every action, irrespective of the time-relation in which it stands with other phenomena, is the immediate effect of the intelligible character of pure reason, which, consequently, enjoys freedom of action, and is not dynamically determined either by internal or external preceding conditions. This freedom must not be described, in a merely negative manner, as independence of empirical conditions, for in this case the faculty of reason would cease to be a cause of phenomena; but it must be regarded, positively, as a faculty which can spontaneously originate a series of events. At the same time, it must not be supposed that any beginning can take place in reason; on the contrary, reason, as the unconditioned condition of all action of the will, admits of no time-conditions, although its effect does really begin in a series of phenomena—a beginning which is not, however, absolutely primal.[1]

If we are scientists then we study mechanical things. If we study humans as empirical scientists then we will view humans mechanically as well. *Whatever* we study as empirical scientists will be mechanical according to us. That is just how empirical science works. But if we look at humans as reasoning beings then we do not view them mechanically. Then they become spontaneous to us. Why? Reasoning is not an empirical phenomenon. It is something free. Kant illustrates this by an example:

> I shall illustrate this regulative principle of reason by an example, from its employment in the world of experience; proved it cannot be by any amount of experience, or by any number of facts, for such arguments cannot establish the truth of transcendental propositions. Let us take a voluntary action—for example, a falsehood—by means of which a man has introduced a certain degree of confusion into the social life of humanity, which is judged according to the motives from which it originated, and the blame of which and of the evil consequences arising from it, is imputed to the offender. We at first proceed to examine the empirical character of the offence, and for this purpose we endeavour to penetrate to the sources of that character, such as a defective education, bad company, a shameless and wicked disposition, frivolity, and want of reflection—not forgetting also the occasioning causes which prevailed at the moment of the transgression. In this the procedure is exactly the same as that pursued in the investigation of the series of causes which determine a given physical effect. Now, although we believe the action to have been determined by all these circumstances, we

---

[1] *Critique of Pure Reason* A550/B578–A553/B580.

do not the less blame the offender. We do not blame him for his unhappy disposition, nor for the circumstances which influenced him, nay, not even for his former course of life; for we presuppose that all these considerations may be set aside, that the series of preceding conditions may be regarded as having never existed, and that the action may be considered as completely unconditioned in relation to any state preceding, just as if the agent commenced with it an entirely new series of effects. Our blame of the offender is grounded upon a law of reason, which requires us to regard this faculty as a cause, which could have and ought to have otherwise determined the behavior of the culprit, independently of all empirical conditions. This causality of reason we do not regard as a co-operating agency, but as complete in itself. It matters not whether the sensuous impulses favored or opposed the action of this causality, the offence is estimated according to its intelligible character—the offender is decidedly worthy of blame, the moment he utters a falsehood. It follows that we regard reason, in spite of the empirical conditions of the act, as completely free, and therefore, therefore, as in the present case, culpable.[1]

If we blame the liar *then* we do not view him as a puppet on a string. Similarly, if we credit someone with an achievement then we want to say the achievement was up to her. Why? Well, it would be incoherent of us to blame or praise individuals while also thinking that they do *not* make the decisive differences. If we think that the causes are really in their parents' behavior then we should be blaming or praising the *parents*, after all. If, again, it was God who caused a criminal to act badly then it is God whom we should blame, not the criminal. This repeats on every level. *Whoever* we praise or blame must be responsible — or we do not make sense.

But, then, how about if we blame and praise absolutely *nobody*? How about living without viewing anyone as free? Is that not a possibility? It is rather easy to see how it is not, in practice. If a waiter asks you whether you want tea or coffee you cannot only say, "Let us see what happens to me." You must pick. It is either/or. No answer will come from your mouth unless you give it. In other words, nothing will simply happen to you. You are unable to approach your life that way. You are inside your life, not above it.

We can illustrate the same point by means of different examples. You are placed as a chooser when you move in traffic, when you form sentences, etc. Everywhere where you act you must think of yourself as making the essential difference. You choose. "Do I turn here or not?,"

---

[1] *Critique of Pure Reason* A553/B581–A555/B583.

you ask yourself, or "Should I have another drink?" You are at the crossroads.

One may still doubt this. Is it not the case that when you move in traffic, say when you drive, that many of the things you do are not all that intentional? For example, if you have already driven for years then you will not need to concentrate on changing gears. You are so accustomed to changing gears that you just do it right, out of sheer habit. And are there not many other things just like this? You say "Hello" in response to a greeting quite routinely, and without needing to consider in your thoughts, "What should I say to *that?!*" It is ordinary and habitual to greet and to drive in certain ways, and also to do so much else, and one does not need even to think about those things after a certain learning period. One does not need to be dumbfounded *all the time*. Children need to ask why but as adults we are already adapted and functioning. So is Kant not wrong in saying that we face all these choices? Is it not therefore actually open to us to become determinists? Why not, in the end, be an empirical scientist all the time?

Kant does not actually give us very strict guidelines as to *where* the region of agency must reside in every area of ordinary life. But it is plausible to insist that it must exist *somewhere*. For even in the most normal adult life everything cannot be up to habits and customs. Even if one can drive and greet according to routines, one will need to make some decisions. Will one tell the truth to one's friend about her song? Will one go to bed already? Where to go for a holiday? Even if much is swallowed up by habits, everything is not. Alternatively, if everything is swallowed up by habits then one must be housed in a place like a prison or a hospital. Most radically, one will need to pretend that one is dead.

The next thing we need to understand is how Kant thinks of agents as something *internally conflicted*. Compare these situations:

You are afraid of the dark alley you have to walk through alone one night in a wild and restless part of town — but you resolve to be brave and walk through without being spooked by the many little sounds that surround you. That is, you overcome your fear. But now, you could not possibly ever be brave without fearing first. It just would not be courage, and it would not be your achievement, if there were not first that pain of fear that is specifically yours. That is, *both* opposites — the fear and the courage — are needed inside of your *self*, or *you* cannot be credited with a deed. If you are to qualify as a free individual who deserves credit for good actions and criticism for bad ones, then you must be conflicted inside.

You are frustrated with a misbehaving child and feel like pinching her. You have had your fill, she makes you furious. She has gone too far. But instead you give her a big hug. Now, you deserve credit for being kind in this circumstance because you had the real ability also to be cruel. You felt the need, you had the power. And yet you chose. You made the difference. You were in a conflicted self-relation: you were in a *dialectic*. That is exactly where you *had* to be to deserve any merit, or in fact to qualify as anybody at all!

This same thinking applies across the board. If a criminal does not choose to commit crimes then she is innocent. A drug addict is responsible for her lot only if she is not genetically determined to need the drug. A crying child may not be able to stop crying, etc. But *wherever* it is that we have agents and not mere patients we get dialectical selves. So the agents, the selves, are exactly the locations of the dialectics.

Kant does not *say* that all agents' internal conflicts are "dialectical." He does not make that association. He speaks of conflicts in the self, and of the necessity of being able to do otherwise (see the most recent quote above), but not, in this context, of dialectics. This is so though there is no doubt whatever that he values critical self-relations in ethics, saying e.g. that one cannot be brave without overcoming fear, and that one cannot really be kind unless one is capable also of evil, as above. He knows very well what is needed for ethics (better than anybody else does, many a historian of philosophy would say) but he uses other symbols, not the dialectical ones, to describe what it is. So officially Kant holds that there is but a single way to be dialectical, that of the antinomies (and of the paralogisms, which we will come to soon). But in *reality*, *we* know, there are two rather separate kinds of dialectic in Kant, and only one consists of the dead ends of the antinomies (and paralogisms). The other dialectic has a much more positive value also in Kant's eyes. He places a very high value on choice.

But Kant's ethics actually only *begins* from choice. He wants to build on that basis. Fundamentally, what agents have to choose between are two options, autonomy and heteronomy. Now let us move on to them.

3.3. Autonomy and Heteronomy

This is from Kant's *Fundamental Principles of the Metaphysic of Morals:*

> The will is a kind of causality belonging to living beings in so far as they are rational, and freedom would be this property of such causality that it can be efficient, independently on foreign causes determining it; just as physical necessity is the property that the

causality of all irrational beings has of being determined to activity by the influence of foreign causes.

The preceding definition of freedom is negative, and therefore unfruitful for the discovery of its essence; but it leads to a positive conception which is so much the more full and fruitful. Since the conception of causality involves that of laws, according to which, by something that we call cause, something else, namely, the effect, must be produced; hence, although freedom is not a property of the will depending on physical laws, yet it is not for that reason lawless; on the contrary, it must be a causality acting according to immutable laws, but of a peculiar kind; otherwise a free will would be an absurdity. Physical necessity is a heteronomy of the efficient causes, for every effect is possible only according to this law, that something else determines the efficient cause to exert its causality. What else then can freedom of the will be but autonomy, that is the property of the will to be a law to itself?[1]

Freedom is not *only* something unbound, like choice, Kant is saying. Rather, freedom is something which binds itself. It makes its own laws. This is "autonomy." (*Auto* for self and *nomy* for law, from the Greek.) Kant says that the only way that you can be consistent with yourself is by being autonomous. The alternative is "heteronomy," which means self-division. It is a state of disharmony. Then what drives you is not *you*, but something else. Then you are already a little like a puppet, because there are strings attached to you. One string suffices. If something pulls you and it is not you who does the pulling then already you get heteronomy.

Kant says that each autonomous self needs to formulate its own *program* and then to stay true to that program in his actions. This is like acting as a legislator, or like a kind of monarch in one's own kingdom. It is to be a king (or queen) in a country in which one is the only citizen! For if one is autonomous then one is both the source of laws and the only person to need to obey those laws. This is because the autonomous agent commands himself and obeys himself exactly. That is what being autonomous boils down to. It is to preach and practice one and the same thing. It is to be in a coherent self-relation.

Is this dialectical? Once again, Kant does not say it is. "Dialectical" is not his word for it. But there seems again to be a dialectical pattern here that can be deciphered. It is a process in time. First, in the beginning of the process, we would have heteronomy, that is internal conflict. Second, at the end of the process, we would have autonomy, that is a consistent self-relation. (Autonomy is self-relational in the sense of

---

[1] Pp. 65–66.

...zRz, not of ...zRR; for in autonomy one rules over oneself, so z *rules* (= R) z. z does not rule over ruling, as in ...zRR.) Finally, in between the left and the right, that is between the heteronymous beginning and the autonomous ending, we would have — what? Choice. Hence choosing would be a kind of intermediate-level version of the ruling relation (R), as it were the man in the Heraclitean triplet baby : man : god. Heteronomy would be the low-level version of the same relation, that is the baby. And autonomy would be the highpoint, that is the god.

But now let us go back to what Kant himself says.

Kant holds that in autonomy one finds not only freedom but also, at the same time, reason and morality. In other words, if one reasons then one will certainly be kind, he says. Conversely, if someone is unkind then that is a sure sign that she is irrational. Why?

Kant says that the laws which the autonomous need to make for themselves must apply, in their own eyes, to *everyone equally.* This is his main move from reason to morals. For instance, if you make a law for yourself which says "Every day be sure to learn something new!," then you must hold, says Kant, that *everyone should* follow this same law. Kant does not mean that you need to make sure that everyone *does* follow that law. And he does not say that you need to find others agreeing with your law. The majority does not need to vote with you. He says only that you need to act as if you were everyone's king or queen. That is, you need to *pretend* that you are the master of the universe and that all intelligent beings everywhere are citizens of your nation. Then you are autonomous.

Why should one pretend like that? Kant's thought is that this pretence raises your feelings to an *impartial* level. You then consider, "What if everyone did that?" If you lie you are to consider what would happen if *everyone* lied. This, that you consider your own behavior as on a par with everyone else's behavior makes you impartial. You are capable of looking at things from an impartial point of view.

You are unkind and irrational, according to this manner of thinking, if you favor yourself. If you are a special case in traffic, for instance, then you will not be fair to the other drivers. You will apply different rules to them than you do to yourself. But if you say, conversely, that the same laws apply to everyone then you are being fair. This is how Kant sees morals.

This brings us to Kant's "Categorical Imperative." This is a command that tells you to treat other reasoning selves in a way in which you would like to be treated. This command is "categorical" in being unconditional. It contrasts with "hypothetical" imperatives which command only conditionally, saying, "*If* x happens, *then* do y!" Categorical commands say: "Do y, *no matter what!*" The Categorical Imperative is very similar to the Golden Rule, of course. Kant thinks that what he provides is rational backing for an ethos that has been lived by in different regions for millennia.[1]

As a final point about autonomy, we need to be careful not to confuse it with choice. Kant thinks of selfhood and freedom on *two different* levels. On one level he sees us as choosers, and when we choose to choose we step up and take responsibility. But on another level Kant says that we can find our real selves only once we get over our conflicts, divisions, and choices, and command ourselves. The dynamics of Kantian ethics consist of movements between these two levels. One rises to reason, by choice, and then commands, and then obeys; or else one sinks to heteronomy and has no idea who one really is. In the heteronymous state choices multiply but selves are hard to find. It is like a jungle. The commander's post is like a fort in the jungle, or a tower in the fort.

3.4 The Paralogisms

As one ages one begins to have a history of actions and wishes, and one's plans begin in time to repeat. Change is no longer constant. In this way one comes to believe that one already is someone, in a stable way. It is as if one were in a place of one's own. But the truth remains, Kant teaches, that one has no territory in the real world at all. The reality is only, Kant says, that the self is always placed on the razor's edge. One is never safely inside the fort or tower, to use the same metaphor as above, and one always has one foot in the jungle. The choices never end. One is never anything more stable than a chooser. Every day one begins anew.

---

[1] At this point one may note in what way Kant's ideal is logically weaker than Socrates'. A categorical imperative is a rule that applies necessarily, that is without any if's or but's. It fits everywhere. But it is not, even for Kant himself, *sufficient* for a rational self. For whatever rule or law you make for yourself, as a follower of Kant, that rule or law does not need to be your *only* or *main* one. You can list plenty of others. You do not need to pinpoint yourself anywhere. But if you follow Socrates then you *do* need to pinpoint yourself. For your final definition will be your only one! It is where your self-knowledge crystallizes! So in Socrates the self-made rule or law is necessary *and* sufficient. The *whole* self is squeezed into it. Socrates' rationalism is more radical than Kant's in this way.
But one should not think that Socratic selves need to be *dogmatic* for this reason. For in Socrates there is a lengthy process of *searching* for the self. There is dialectical trial and error. So one is not simply to declare, out of the blue, what or who one is. Rather, the topic is a life-long object of study. This is the "examined life," see Chapter 2.

Kant's "paralogisms" are errors of reasoning in this vein.[1] They are those kinds of reasoning that make the self mistake itself for something it is not, namely for a metaphysical reality instead of an ethical task.

Kant has four paralogisms in the *Critique of Pure Reason*, and they may be labeled thus:

objectivity,
simplicity,
personality, and
immateriality (immortality).[2]

Now let us look at each of these in turn.

I. In the *first* paralogism a thinking subject takes itself to be more than a thinking subject. It views itself also as a thought-of object. But it is not an object, Kant says. It is only a subject. It thinks about things but it does not belong among those things which it can think about. Why not? Because thought is always only something that *accompanies* other things. It is nothing *alone*. If you think about apples, you get thought plus apples. If you think about oranges then you get thought plus oranges. But if you subtract the apples and the oranges and want

---

[1] This is not exactly the background that Kant provides for the paralogisms in the *Critique of Pure Reason*. Kant comes to the paralogisms rather from a perspective which presupposes familiarity with Descartes, Leibniz, Wolff, and/or Mendelssohn (and perhaps Plato's *Phaedo*). But in this book it cannot be assumed that the reader is familiar with those sources, so a different background is necessary.
Also, Kant comes to the paralogisms *before* the antinomies, unlike his book. But the antinomies seem to be better to present first because they are more approachable. They are something every child could be brought to understand, one feels, for by a certain age virtually everyone seems to have thought of questions about the limits of the universe and the beginnings of time. But few seem to consider how subjects and objects or egos and essences get mixed up.
Would it not have been worthwhile to describe Descartes etc. before coming to Kant? There is a different reason for this. Many of the Cartesian associations about private egos are irrelevant to the dialectics of this book. In this book there is recurrently a conflict between the *ought* and the *is*, or the free agent and the determined patient. This is roughly the conflict between Socrates and Plato, the Kantian subject and the Kantian object, and Marx's creative labor and modern machinery. Descartes' mind/body dualism is not analogous to these other dualities. For an introduction to Descartes see Kenny.
[2] Kant's own titles for his four paralogisms are: substantiality, simplicity, personality, and ideality. I have reasons for not using the first and the last of these. Talk of "substances" may not be familiar to modern readers who do not already know of the Aristotelian tradition. But such talk is better to avoid in this book, as it would often confuse. "Ideality," again, sounds too much like ethics. For one may think that if a self is "ideal" then it is *alright*, by Kant's lights. But now Kant means by "ideality" something metaphysical and not something ethical. It is better simply to not use multi-purpose words.

to have only thought then you have absolutely nothing. In other words, thought, or the self, is for Kant only something like a shadow. There is a shadow of a tree, and a shadow of a bus, but if you want a shadow plain and simple, that is a shadow that is not a shadow of some particular thing, then you get nothing. The shadow *per se is* nothing.

Of course this first paralogism is something quite strange, given that our selves or thoughts (or wills, etc.) are capable of choices or autonomy, etc. Shadows do not make choices, of course, and shadows are very far from something autonomous or self-sufficient! They are precisely *de*pendent, not independent. So definitely we are not *altogether* like shadows. And so Kant's first paralogism is certainly something puzzling.

But let us move on to get a fuller picture of Kant's paralogisms before we clarify his meaning.

II. The *second* paralogism occurs when the I or the ego takes itself to be a simple and continuous thing. This is merely to go further than the first paralogism. Now the I does not only exist, as an object which can be thought about. It also has a very basic characteristic, namely that it is individual, or indivisible. It is, metaphysically, like the property yellow, which spreads to the bananas and lemons of the world, for example. It is like a thin layer that covers a range of objects. The I is felt to be indivisible, like yellow is, in that it is not complex. It is not formed from other things. For instance the color orange you would get from mixing yellow and red, but yellow you do not get by means of any mixing operation. You need to have it from the beginning or you will not have it at all. You do not get it from any other thing. It is basic, it is archetypal — it is its own kind of thing.

But this thinking, too, is wrong, Kant says. What is the mistake this time? Well, you do see yellow, and you see bananas and lemons, but you never see yourself. Similarly, you hear the birds, and you hear the traffic, but the self? No. You do not have contacts with the self through any of your senses. So you have no evidence of its simplicity, Kant says.

Again we should pause. It sounds alarming if one's individuality is questioned. One *feels* like someone, does one not? And one does *speak* for oneself, is that not so? Are these not evidence? And is it not necessary in any case for a chooser to be some one source of action? Certainly if one is nothing at all then one cannot choose, any more than one can walk or fly. ("Nothing comes out of nothing," as Shakespeare says.) So is Kant not wrong about the imperceptibility of the ego? That does not seem so either. And yet there *is* no evidence of us like there is of lemons and bananas. So he is right about that. And hence it seems that we are caught in a bind.

III. The *third* paralogism says one has a self-identity. There is some place and some time where one begins and another where one ends, and one lives between those points. One has external bounds in that way. Moreover, there is something that one is within. One can move back and forth in the tunnel. One remembers one's past experiences and past thoughts as one's own; and when one plans for the future one often comes to realize, in the future, how one's own earlier plan was a good one or a bad one. In general, one routinely considers oneself to be the same person through time. Perhaps one changes sometimes but the rule is that one stays the same, on an underlying level.

Now what is wrong with this? Kant says that persons *need* to think of themselves, normally, as consistent individuals but that they do not, and cannot, base their demands or assertions of continuity on any *evidence*. There is only a demand for continuity, inside each of us, and then we insist that the continuity is there. We do not *find out* that it is there, Kant says. We just *need* it.

Again one should react with dissatisfaction on hearing what Kant says. After all, it sounds incredible that we do not have identities. Of course we have beginnings and endings somewhere, even if we cannot show or say where exactly those are. *Every* thing has its place, of course. So why not we?

Kant is saying that this is because we are self-*made*. We are not like objects. We do not simply *find* ourselves. If we pretend to find ourselves then we are belittling ourselves.

For example, if I say that I have always loved the music of Coltrane then I can be right about my stable taste in jazz. It can be that I happen to like a certain class of jazz melodies and rhythms more than others, in a constant way through time. But I am demeaning myself if I say I am only or mainly or essentially a jazz lover. What *I* am is an *agent*; I am not only someone with regular tastes and habits.

My *pet* can have a personality in that demeaned sense — if, that is, it is purely a slave to its habits and inclinations. Then it would follow that my pet does not choose or reason. Do I know it does not? How can I tell? Kant is saying that you cannot tell. There is no evidence about agents, ever. (You and I and all agents are in this way "secret agents." We are *noumena*, not *phenomena*, in Kant's words.) You *choose* to view your pet either way, that is all.

Do we face a similar choice about ourselves? *No*, Kant says. We are stuck in the choosing mode. If we try to seem only like pets then we are pretending. Then we are choosing behind the scenes. We cannot *really* choose not to choose. It is remarkably easy to conceal one's choosing capability, Kant says. Compare this anecdote from a recent author:

> In an old Eastern European joke, a man is urged to stop obeying his wife in every matter and to start following his own free will, whereupon he replies that he *always* follows his own judgment, as freely as everyone, and it so happens that his own judgment tells him to ask his wife what to do and follow her advice.[1] (Italics in original.)

The trick to concealing oneself as a chooser is to pick an authority to obey consistently. One can then *hide behind* that authority, pretending to be no one. The man in this joke chooses to obey his wife. But one could also elect to obey, say, astrological cards. (And we have already mentioned hospitals and prisons, with their routines or authorities.)[2]

Now we turn to the final paralogism.

IV. The *fourth* paralogism is that the self is immaterial. You can abstract yourself from one kind of material and also from another kind of material, and then you begin to suspect that you could be abstracted from all materials altogether, and this makes you think that you could live after your body dies, as a spirit or soul. For example, you can imagine yourself without legs, without teeth, even without a face. You can separate yourself, in your thoughts, from so much. The only thing you cannot separate yourself from is your thinking. So, it is tempting to conclude, you *are* that thinker. That is where you are. The thinker always comes along, no matter where you go.

Kant objects to this that you are never entitled to conclude that you would still remain if *no* materials remained. All the thinking you have done has in fact been while being attached to your body. Even when you imagine things you remain connected to your body. You have not in fact tried living without your body. You do not know that you can do it.

This fourth paralogism is perhaps the least dramatic, in that Kant claims the least in it. He does not say that he can show that we have no immortal souls. He says only that we cannot show that we do have immortal souls if we argue as he says. In other words, Kant is not

---

[1] Arpaly p. 175.

[2] The point of the joke from Arpaly is somewhat different, of course. In it the man claims that he is a free chooser though he seems always to obey his wife. He claims, in effect, to *consider independently* each of his wife's choices before obeying them. He is laughed at because it is suspected that he does not do any of that independent considering. He submits blindly to his wife, the laughers suspect, though he claims to be more dignified. In a word, he does *not* hide behind his wife, as one would in a Kantian scenario. Rather, he pretends that he has something *to* hide.

preaching materialism. He is trying to make metaphysical skeptics of us. This opens the way for our activities, he believes. For the world is not a ready-made place. Things will go right only if we do them. Our own activity is crucial. This is Kant's strange world. It does not consist only of real objects but also of eternally incomplete subjects, who act without any compulsion.

Now we have surveyed all of the four paralogisms. Here is a short generalization from Kant about the kind of mistake he is guiding us away from by means of his paralogisms:

The logical exposition of thought in general is mistaken for a metaphysical determination of the object.[1]

Thoughts occur in processes, but objects are something very different from these. Dialectic is a human need, not a hallmark of reality. Kant's paralogisms underline this difference. We know objects empirically, not by reasoning. We should not try to reason about reality — not even our own reality — but only about ideals. We have seen that it is tempting to think otherwise. One easily slips into thinking that one has some kind of a special access to an underlying reality based merely on one's thought. Kant's conclusion is that it just does not exist. There is no *place* for our thoughts.

The temptation is supposed to be especially great to *dialecticians*. This is so according to Kant. He believes that dialectical patterns of thought lead us to reason about reality not only as in the antinomies but also as in the paralogisms. Dialectical reasoning regularly oversteps the bounds that properly belong to reasoning. Or, to put the same point in more positive terms, dialecticians do not understand what reasoning really is good for. They should be using it to form plans of action.

As before, one needs to take Kant's remarks on dialectics with some salt. It is not exactly correct to say that dialecticians reason about realities and not about ideals. For we have already seen that Socrates and Plato reason also about ideals. After all, in Socrates self-predication and self-knowledge were ideals, and in Plato the Good was an ideal. These were not given realities for them. Rather, they were ethical tasks. Hence, Kant's negative generalization about dialectics is mistaken — once again. The errors Kant finds in reasoning are not characteristically dialectical, just as the new and positive directions that he guides us to are not specifically anti-dialectical or non-dialectical! He mistakes dialectic for his enemy. It is not.

But Kant's mistaken generalizations about dialectics do not need to take away the value of his paralogisms. They remain instructive.

---

[1] *Critique of Pure Reason* A408.

The paralogisms' point is to teach us to avoid vain objectifications, whoever it is that makes them. If we objectify ourselves then we make ourselves stiff like mummies. If we think of ourselves as constant things with stable characters then we will hold ourselves back from the free and autonomous processes that are really open to us. For in practice our supposedly neutral descriptions of ourselves will translate into promises to stay the same, which is never in our real interest, and which could never correspond with our actual capabilities. In Chapter 4 we will see how Marx continues along similar lines.

Now what remains for us to discuss is Kant's relation to Plato.

3.5 Kant's Plato

On the face of it, Kant's view of Plato is surprisingly sympathetic and understanding, given that he certainly knows Plato to be a major dialectician and metaphysician. Here are some of Kant's large generalizations about Plato in the *Critique of Pure Reason:*

> Plato employed the expression idea in a way that plainly showed he meant by it something which is never derived from the senses, but which far transcends even the conceptions of the understanding (with which Aristotle occupied himself), inasmuch as in experience nothing perfectly corresponding to them could be found. Ideas are, according to him, archetypes of things themselves, and not merely keys to possible experiences, like the categories. In his view they flow from the highest reason, by which they have been imparted to human reason, which, however, exists no longer in its original state, but is obliged with great labor to recall by reminiscence—which is called philosophy—the old but now sadly obscured ideas. I will not here enter upon any literary investigation of the sense which this sublime philosopher attached to this expression. I shall content myself with remarking that it is nothing unusual, in common conversation as well as in written works, by comparing the thoughts which an author has delivered upon a subject, to understand him better than he understood himself inasmuch as he may not have sufficiently determined his conception, and thus have sometimes spoken, nay even thought, in opposition to his own opinions.
>
> Plato perceived very clearly that our faculty of cognition has the feeling of a much higher vocation than that of merely spelling out phenomena according to synthetical unity, for the purpose of being able to read them as experience, and that our reason naturally raises itself to cognitions far too elevated to admit of the possibility of

an object given by experience corresponding to them—cognitions which are nevertheless real, and are not mere phantoms of the brain.[1]

Kant has now said that Plato is a rationalist, trusting thought more than experience. Also, Plato's "ideas," which we called Forms or Ideas, are something self-sufficient, unlike Aristotle's categories. (To clarify, Aristotle's categories are like widely applicable tools for thought. These are not applied to themselves. In contrast, Plato's theoretic objects — the "ideas," or Ideas — are not only tools for thinking about *other* things. Rather they are primarily the independent *ends* of thought. They are about and for *themselves*.)

But Kant has now suggested also that Plato may not have understood himself best. What does Kant mean by that?

> This philosopher found his ideas especially in all that is practical, that is, which rests upon freedom, which in its turn ranks under cognitions that are the peculiar product of reason. He who would derive from experience the conceptions of virtue, who would make (as many have really done) that, which at best can but serve as an imperfectly illustrative example, a model for or the formation of a perfectly adequate idea on the subject, would in fact transform virtue into a nonentity changeable according to time and circumstance and utterly incapable of being employed as a rule. On the contrary, everyone is conscious that, when anyone is held up to him as a model of virtue, he compares this so-called model with the true original which he possesses in his own mind and values him according to this standard. But this standard is the idea of virtue, in relation to which all possible objects of experience are indeed serviceable as examples—proofs of the practicability in a certain degree of that which the conception of virtue demands—but certainly not as archetypes. That the actions of man will never be in perfect accordance with all the requirements of the pure ideas of reason, does not prove the thought to be chimerical. For only through this idea are all judgments as to moral merit or demerit possible; it consequently lies at the foundation of every approach to moral perfection, however far removed from it the obstacles in human nature—indeterminable as to degree—may keep us.[2]

Kant is saying that as free agents we *need* things like the "ideas." For freedom is not an empirical phenomenon. It is missing from the natural world, as the antinomies showed (see especially the Third Antithesis). Moreover, we need to be guided by things that are superior to ourselves:

> The Platonic Republic has become proverbial as an example— and a striking one—of imaginary perfection, such as can exist only

---

[1] *Critique of Pure Reason* A312/B368–A314/370.
[2] *Critique of Pure Reason* A314/B370–A3167372.

in the brain of the idle thinker; and Brucker ridicules the philosopher for maintaining that a prince can never govern well, unless he is participant in the ideas. But we should do better to follow up this thought and, where this admirable thinker leaves us without assistance, employ new efforts to place it in clearer light, rather than carelessly fling it aside as useless, under the very miserable and pernicious pretext of impracticability. A constitution of the greatest possible human freedom according to laws, by which the liberty of every individual can consist with the liberty of every other (not of the greatest possible happiness, for this follows necessarily from the former), is, to say the least, a necessary idea, which must be placed at the foundation not only of the first plan of the constitution of a state, but of all its laws. And, in this, it not necessary at the outset to take account of the obstacles which lie in our way—obstacles which perhaps do not necessarily arise from the character of human nature, but rather from the previous neglect of true ideas in legislation. For there is nothing more pernicious and more unworthy of a philosopher, than the vulgar appeal to a so-called adverse experience, which indeed would not have existed, if those institutions had been established at the proper time and in accordance with ideas; while, instead of this, conceptions, crude for the very reason that they have been drawn from experience, have marred and frustrated all our better views and intentions. The more legislation and government are in harmony with this idea, the more rare do punishments become and thus it is quite reasonable to maintain, as Plato did, that in a perfect state no punishments at all would be necessary. Now although a perfect state may never exist, the idea is not on that account the less just, which holds up this maximum as the archetype or standard of a constitution, in order to bring legislative government always nearer and nearer to the greatest possible perfection. For at what precise degree human nature must stop in its progress, and how wide must be the chasm which must necessarily exist between the idea and its realization, are problems which no one can or ought to determine— and for this reason, that it is the destination of freedom to overstep all assigned limits between itself and the idea.[1]

We need things to aim at which we have not yet attained. Even if we cannot ever attain them completely we need to approach them as nearly as possible. As free agents we should "overstep all assigned limits" in seeking them.

But Kant also finds *faults* in Plato's philosophy:

But not only in that wherein human reason is a real causal agent and where ideas are operative causes (of actions and their objects), that is to say, in the region of ethics, but also in regard to nature

---

[1] *Critique of Pure Reason* A316/B372–A317/B373.

herself, Plato saw clear proofs of an origin from ideas. A plant, and animal, the regular order of nature—probably also the disposition of the whole universe—give manifest evidence that they are possible only by means of and according to ideas; that, indeed, no one creature, under the individual conditions of its existence, perfectly harmonizes with the idea of the most perfect of its kind—just as little as man with the idea of humanity, which nevertheless he bears in his soul as the archetypal standard of his actions; that, notwithstanding, these ideas are in the highest sense individually, unchangeably, and completely determined, and are the original causes of things; and that the totality of connected objects in the universe is alone fully adequate to that idea. Setting aside the exaggerations of expression in the writings of this philosopher, the mental power exhibited in this ascent from the ectypal mode of regarding the physical world to the architectonic connection thereof according to ends, that is, ideas, is an effort which deserves imitation and claims respect. But as regards the principles of ethics, of legislation, and of religion, spheres in which ideas alone render experience possible, although they never attain to full expression therein, he has vindicated for himself a position of peculiar merit, which is not appreciated only because it is judged by the very empirical rules, the validity of which as principles is destroyed by ideas. For as regards nature, experience presents us with rules and is the source of truth, but in relation to ethical laws experience is the parent of illusion, and it is in the highest degree reprehensible to limit or to deduce the laws which dictate what I ought to do, from what is done.[1]

In this piece of text we find the hallmarks of a Kantian interpretation of Plato. The rationalism is valuable when it is ethical, but not when it is cosmological.

Kant also assigns Plato a prominent position in his *antinomies*.

Both Epicurus and Plato assert more in their systems than they know. The former encourages and advances science—although to the prejudice of the practical; the latter presents us with excellent principles for the investigation of the practical, but, in relation to everything regarding which we can attain to speculative cognition, permits reason to append idealistic explanations of natural phenomena, to the great injury of physical investigation.[2]

Epicurus is the ancient empiricist who sides with the antitheses in Kant's antinomies. Plato is on the side of the theses, besides being the superior ethician. Epicurus is strong on science and weak on ideals. Plato, on the other hand, is strong on ideals and weak on experience

---

[1] *Critique of Pure Reason* A317/B373–A317/B374.
[2] *Critique of Pure Reason* A471/B499.

or experiment. Plato is the archetypal "Dogmatist," while Epicurus is the original "Empiricist." Here are some of Kant's main generalizations about these two sides to the traditional disputes:

On the side of Dogmatism, or of the thesis, therefore, in the determination of the cosmological ideas, we find:

1. A practical interest, which must be very dear to every right-thinking man. That the world has a beginning—that the nature of my thinking self is simple, and therefore indestructible—that I am a free agent, and raised above the compulsion of nature and her laws—and, finally, that the entire order of things, which form the world, is dependent upon a Supreme Being, from whom the whole receives unity and connection—these are so many foundation-stones of morality and religion. The antithesis deprives us of all these supports—or, at least, seems so to deprive us.

2. A speculative interest of reason manifests itself on this side. For, if we take the transcendental ideas and employ them in the manner which the thesis directs, we can exhibit completely a priori the entire chain of conditions, and understand the derivation of the conditioned—beginning from the unconditioned. This the antithesis does not do; and for this reason does not meet with so welcome a reception. For it can give no answer to our question respecting the conditions of its synthesis—except such as must be supplemented by another question, and so on to infinity. According to it, we must rise from a given beginning to one still higher; every part conducts us to a still smaller one; every event is preceded by another event which is its cause; and the conditions of existence rest always upon other and still higher conditions, and find neither end nor basis in some self-subsistent thing as the primal being. [...]

On the side of the antithesis, or Empiricism, in the determination of the cosmological ideas:

1. We cannot discover any such practical interest arising from pure principles of reason as morality and religion present. On the contrary, pure empiricism seems to empty them of all their power and influence. If there does not exist a Supreme Being distinct from the world—if the world is without beginning, consequently without a Creator—if our wills are not free, and the soul is divisible and subject to corruption just like matter—the ideas and principles of morality lose all validity and fall with the transcendental ideas which constituted their theoretical support.

2. But empiricism, in compensation, holds out to reason, in its speculative interests, certain important advantages, far exceeding any that the dogmatist can promise us. For, when employed by the empiricist, understanding is always upon its proper ground of investigation—the field of possible experience, the laws of which it

can explore, and thus extend its cognition securely and with clear intelligence without being stopped by limits in any direction.[1]

Kant feels the pull of both sides, but not exactly in the same matters. He sees the value of Plato's philosophy for ethics and Epicurus' for science. In this way Kant manages to find a consistent position for himself. He can follow Plato more on values and Epicurus more on facts. Because there is a gap between values and facts — that is, a gap between what ought to be and what is — there is no inconsistency in the overall position that Kant adopts. In other words, both sides, the rationalistic and the empiricistic, can be right — if they do not aim for the same things.[2]

But is Kant's domesticated Plato tenable? This is *Plato light*, is it not? Is that OK? What can be said about that?

In Kant Plato appears to be identified in a marvelously coherent and realistic way. Plato, or the ethical aspect of Plato, seems to be adapted to modern life almost comfortably. We can have a scientific world-view, Kant says, and we can still evaluate free actions by Plato's high standards.

Is this satisfactory? Well, not entirely. We saw already that Kant ignores the self-relational character of dialectics. On one level this is a point about Plato. Plato is not so much for finitude, as Kant's "Dogmatist" is, as for *self-relations*. The self-relations may mark finite bounds or infinite excesses. For Plato says *both* of these things, as we already saw in Chapter 2. A self-moving God in the *Laws* acts at a finite point in time. Hence, the God's act is unique. It does not extend, and it does not repeat. In contrast, the Forms or Ideas in the *Phaedo* are, besides something self-predicated, infinite, so they do stretch through time. It is just not correct to put Plato in too small of a box. Plato is not always on the side of Kant's theses.

But it is also important to keep in mind that this focus on self-relations is not only *Plato's*. There is something *dialectical* about it, which Kant misses. I already mentioned other self-relations in

---

[1] *Critique of Pure Reason* A465/B493–A467/B495.
[2] One should not forget, however, that Kant is *not* entitling empirical science to solve such big mysteries as the origins of the universe or the nature of time. In recent history astronomers and theorists of Einsteinian relativity have often over-stepped these bounds. The Big Bang, for example, tends to be taken seriously today by many not only as a theory that is relativized to the limitations and assumptions of empirical inquiry, but absolutely (and it is ironic that the very idea of a Big Bang is *opposed* to Kant's empiricist anti-theses; but let us not go into that here). For an introduction to some recent physical theories with ambitions that are excessive from a Kantian viewpoint, see Greene.

dialectics: the Hindu *Atman*, Descartes' *Cogito*, Hegel's *Geist*, Marx's *labor*. The history of dialectical thinking is predominantly self-critical and self-conscious, so it is not in general like Kant's pairs of theses and antitheses or like his paralogisms. What distinguishes dialecticians is not that they try to end relational series abruptly, in a form like aRbRc... xRz. If they ended their series in such sudden and seemingly arbitrary ways then they would deserve the kinds of objections that they get in Kant's antinomies. But they do not. Therefore the objections miss their targets. Moreover, it is not typical of dialecticians to make of selves metaphysical objects instead of ethical ideals. We know that many dialectics are actually ethical projects, so Kant's paralogisms are not representative of dialectics in general.[1]

Perhaps the focal point of all dialectical protests against Kant is that dialectic is, instead of the "logic of illusion," the logic of free and creative agents! We saw in Chapter 1 that already Heraclitus' patterns seemed to point in this direction, and Socrates and Plato took the same thinking further in Chapter 2. And then, in this chapter, Chapter 3, we have noted a few times how Kant's own positive and ethical and freedom-friendly positions are actually dialectical though he does not say so.

A different basis for questioning Kant's reconstruction of Plato is by premising on the value of *dialogue*. Dialogue is, of course, Plato's mode of expression, and we saw in the Introduction how easy it is to shape dialectics in dialogues. But this is not Kant's mode. Kant is more of a solitary thinker. He seems not to consider seriously the possibility that our selves or egos might be reflected in what we say to each other when we meet (or in writing, from a distance). Socrates and Plato regularly assume that language has the power to reveal souls or egos.[2] This opens up the possibility of formulating and polishing different thought processes in public life, sincerely with others. In contrast, Kant shows us antinomies and paralogisms and then leaves us with our private intuitions to construct whatever ethical laws we may feel are right, as if our projects had to be individualistic.[3]

---

[1] But, some readers may say, must one not forgive Kant, who wrote after Descartes, Leibniz, and Wolff? Is Kant not alright in the light of his own historical experience? Well, not about *Plato*, or about *dialectics*. If we are too nice to Kant then we are unfair to Plato.
[2] At *Charmides* 159A Socrates says that a thought or soul is revealed by saying what is meant. At *Sophist* 263E thought altogether is silent speech or inner dialogue. On the other hand, in the *Seventh Letter* language can *not* express the essential truth (344B–C).
[3] Habermas attaches great importance to this.

But this is not to criticize *everything* in Kant. His essential insights may still remain correct. Perhaps reasoning really does belong only to ethics and not to metaphysics. If it does then Zeno should not be thinking about running or arrows so much as about thought; Heraclitus should not focus on God as much as on his own logical standards; Plato would do better to not think of the Forms as real; etc. All these energies that have been directed at studying life as it is should actually be directed at improving it. Kant may be correct in this for the reasons that we have studied in this chapter.

Marx would agree with that conclusion. He says:

> The philosophers have only interpreted the world, in various ways; the point is to change it.[1]

Now let us move on to his philosophy.

Further Reading

Frederick C. Beiser: *German Idealism.* This book introduces to the thought of Kant and his immediate followers. It is rich with information but its formulations are always simple.

Immanuel Kant: *Critique of Judgment.* This is Kant's last major work, and it is not the easiest to approach. The two works below should be studied first. But this last one is the climax of the Kantian story, for this is where everything begins to fit together. (Agents and patients still stand apart and opposed in the earlier books, but not in this final one.)

Immanuel Kant: *Critique of Pure Reason.* There is enough to study in this work for a lifetime. It is rare in being lucid as well as important. (Often one finds that exact scholarly work does not reveal anything important to life, and on the other hand that the great issues of life are presented as matters of taste; but with Kant there is neither problem.)

Immanuel Kant: *Fundamental Principles of the Metaphysic of Morals.* This is the easiest to read of all of Kant's books.

(See the Bibliography at the end of this book for detailed information on these and other titles.)

---

[1] Thesis XI in the "Theses on Feuerbach."

CHAPTER 4. MARX

Vor ihren Geschöpfen haben sie, die Schöpfer, sich gebeugt.
(German for: *They, the creators, have bowed down before their creations.*)

— Marx

Karl Marx's time is not much later than Kant's, but socially the period is already very different. The Industrial Revolution has become effective especially in England, where Marx spends much of his mature life, and it has lead to the formation of new urban centers with problems of poverty, child labor, pollution, etc. Moreover, with the German Idealists after Kant idealistic philosophy seems to have gone mad. The systems of Fichte, Schelling, and Hegel follow each other quickly and make the boldest claims. In general, by Marx's time the optimism of Kant's Enlightenment has already declined. Human reason is looked upon with more suspicion than hope.

What does Marx do in this situation? He retains some of the older humanistic values, in that he is for the *free self-expression* of all through creative action, and this is something I will begin this chapter with. Self-expression goes wrong in one way when "fetishism" occurs. This is very much like idolatry, as idolatry is described in the Old Testament or Hebrew Bible.

But Marx also changes something. He, too, makes his revolution in dialectical thought. He turns from idealism to *materialism*. Marx believes, for one thing, that the material world runs its course quite independently of our wills. More radically, he holds that the material world tends to determine our wills! In other words, minds are controlled by matter. This is materialism. This is the opposite of what we found Plato and Kant to say. Plato and Kant are idealists, saying that mind controls matter, but Marx is a materialist, holding the opposite view.

Now one might ask: Is materialism contrary to the possibility of free self-expression? Or is Marx inconsistent? The answer is: Marx is consistent. Materialism only complicates the familiar picture. The old picture is not erased: it is added to. Marx says that we need to organize material relations first and then afterwards we can actually come to control matter with our minds in a kind of communistic utopia. So one dialectic needs to precede the other. First in time we need the new materialistic one and then we can come to the old idealistic one.

After showing these things I will compare some "Marxists" to Marx. Engels, Bernstein, Lenin, and Mao all depart from Marx's thinking, and so do so many other powerful agents in the politics of the past century. The heart of the story is that these powerful players recognize only the materialistic dialectic and not the old humanistic one. Hence, the socialisms of the real world became inhumane and technocratic. Therefore they failed to bring Marxian dialectics to life in the real, material world. They took Marx's means and turned these into ends.

4.1 The Humanistic Dialectic

For Marx individuals are creative beings who should be free and self-reliant. But in history things do not normally go this way. We do not live up to our potentials or trust our own creative powers sufficiently. Instead we keep falling back on external objects and authorities. We pretend that these stand above us and that we need to submit to them. What makes the situation particularly ironic is that those external things are our own creations.

One version of this unfreedom in Marx is religious. He says man creates god, not god man. In his words: "They, the creators, have bowed down before their creations." This is ironic, of course. A god made by man is not a real god.

Marx calls this phenomenon "fetishism." What is fetishism? It is the worship of a false god. But it is not necessarily directed only at a god. One can also have fetishism in the market economy, Marx says. Individuals "fetishize" products as if the products had power over the individuals. This happens even though it is only humans who *make* the products. It would be more appropriate to divine the makers. They are really the precious elements in the world — the creators. This is Marx's central message, even if so many socialistic societies in recent history have made it seem otherwise.

Fetishism is a curious phenomenon. It leads us to view things backwards. We place gods or goods above ourselves even though we really should be standing above them. We organize things in such a way that they come to control us and to dominate us. *We organize* things that way, Marx says. So fetishism amounts to a kind of voluntary surrender.

In what sense can goods rule over us? The young Marx says:

> Private property has made us so stupid and partial that an object is only ours when we have it, when it exists for us as capital or when it is directly eaten, drunk, worn, inhabited, etc., in short, utilized in some way. Although private property itself only conceives these various forms of possession as means of life, and the life for which they serve as means is the life of private property — labor and creation of capital. Thus all the physical and intellectual senses have been replaced by the simple alienation of all these senses; the sense of having. The human being had to be reduced to this absolute poverty in order to be able to give birth to all his inner wealth.[1]

In having so much one does nothing. Why so? Because if one has much then one can let others do things for one — by paying them:

> That which is for me through the medium of *money* — that for which I can pay (i.e., which money can buy) — that am I *myself*, the possessor of the money. The extent of the power of money is the extent of my power. Money's properties are my — the possessor's — properties and essential powers. Thus, what I *am* and *am capable of* is by no means determined by my individuality. I *am* ugly, but I can buy for myself the *most beautiful* of women. Therefore I am not *ugly*, for the effect of *ugliness* — its deterrent power — is nullified by money. I, according to my individual characteristics, am *lame*, but money furnishes me with twenty-four feet. Therefore I am not lame. I am bad, dishonest, unscrupulous, stupid; but money is honored, and hence its possessor. Money is the supreme good, therefore its possessor is good. Money, besides, saves me the trouble of being dishonest: I am therefore presumed honest. I am *brainless*, but money is the *real brain* of all things and how then should its possessor be brainless? Besides, he can buy clever people for himself, and is he who has power over the clever not more clever than the clever? Do not I, who thanks to money am capable of *all* that the human heart longs for, possess all human capacities? Does not my money, therefore, transform all my incapacities into their contrary?[2] (Italics in original.)

---

[1] From "Private Property and Communism" in the 1844 manuscripts.
[2] From "The Power of Money" in the 1844 manuscripts.

Your money takes care of things for you, so all you need is money, Marx says ironically. He quotes from Goethe's *Faust* to illustrate the same point:

> What, man! confound it, hands and feet
> And head and backside, all are yours!
> And what we take while life is sweet,
> Is that to be declared not ours?
> Six stallions, say, I can afford,
> Is not their strength my property?
> I tear along, a sporting lord,
> As if their legs belonged to me.

Mephistopheles' irony is, in Marx's words, that "the production of too many useful things results in too many useless people."[1]

Money or property *seems* to extend our powers because it allows us to have more things done for us. But in reality it *impoverishes* us because it leads us to lose our skills.

But is this so bad? Is it so bad to lose skills in making pottery and in farming if one can easily pay for quality goods by means of an office job? Is it such a big sacrifice if one cannot bake one's own bread anymore?

Well, the real trouble begins once goods seem to spread too widely in our lives. For then our incapabilities also begin to be too widespread. We tend not only to rely on useful goods and then to do other things with our friends, for example. Rather, Marx says, goods begin to intertwine with our very friendships! We begin to see goods nearly everywhere. And this leads to disturbing illusions. We lose the sense of reality that Marx is after in the following early excerpt:

> [...] love can only be exchanged for love, trust for trust, etc. If you wish to enjoy art you must be an artistically cultivated person; if you wish to influence other people you must be a person who really has a stimulating and encouraging effect upon others. Every one of your relations to man and to nature must be a *specific expression*, corresponding to the object of your will, of your *real individual* life. If you love without evoking love in return, i.e., if you are not able, by the *manifestation* of yourself as a loving person, to make yourself a *beloved person*, then your love is impotent and a misfortune.[2] (Italics in original.)

If money or property does not distort social relations then the relations will fall into place, Marx is saying. Then things will fit together like they belong. Love will be exchanged for love, as it will not be prostituted. Art will be recognized as art, not as an investment.

---

[1] From "Human Requirements and Division of Labour Under the Rule of Private Property" in the 1844 manuscripts.
[2] Ibid.

Leaders will be supportive of those whom they lead, and not simply rich.

Real values are not tainted with economic thinking. Love, art, and leadership exemplify this. If you view too many things as goods then you will miss out on some real values.

Let us have another look now at these real values. They are something ancient. Many ancients say that things should be returned in kind. "Reap what you sow!" and "Eye for an eye!" are expressions in this vein. This makes some sense, for only a true artist can *appreciate* art. She will have the needed sensibilities. Similarly, only the lover can be loved. The relation is reciprocal and symmetric. You can only get back what you give. (The leadership relation is a little different because it is not symmetric, but it, too, is a reciprocal relation, so it is approximately from the same family of values.) Things must be in tune with their surroundings and with themselves at once. This is Marx's utopia.

This utopia can be described in dialectical terms as follows. Marx's utopia is a world in which individuals act on their real potentials, that is "realize themselves," or express themselves unhindered. Money will then no longer disturb and upset natural markets. Real abilities will rule. If you show talent as a pianist, for example, then you should play the piano — even if you are poor. If you have a great interest in philosophy, and also an ability to think abstractly, then you ought to philosophize — even if you are rich and could pay others to do it for you! You should by no means pay someone to do your main business for you. You should not sit back and watch and let yourself be entertained. Rather, you should take action, because otherwise your "insides" will languish. Your own characteristics and your personality will then remain concealed. Among the rich and among the poor money distorts things in the capitalist system. For whether you are rich or poor you are not doing what you should be doing. (What should you be doing? Living up to your talents.)

Formally the process of the Marxian dialectic is always the same. There is, on the one hand, a value-making subject and on the other a valued object. The dialectical process is from an asymmetry between the subject and object to a symmetry. So there is first a conflict and then a match. The low point in life is for the subject to worship the object, and the high point is for the subject to express herself consciously and therefore to know herself as a creator.

This should sound familiar from the previous chapters. There is a self-relational end: self-expression. And the route to that end is conflicted. In Socrates' terms one might picture this quest of the self as a series of questions which demand a satisfying answer. First the questions receive only frustratingly inadequate answers, and only finally is there an answer with which the questioner can rest. The only difference is that Marx is not saying that the process is dialogical. For Marx self-realization does not happen by means of speech. We will come back to that later.

Here is Marx's central message of emancipation:

> The criticism of religion disillusions man, so that he will think, act, and fashion his reality like a man who has discarded his illusions and regained his senses, so that he will move around himself as his own true Sun. Religion is only the illusory Sun which revolves around man as long as he does not revolve around himself. It is, therefore, the *task of history*, once the *other-world of truth* has vanished, to establish the *truth of this world*. It is the immediate *task of philosophy*, which is in the service of history, to unmask self-estrangement [...].[1]

Man learns eventually to focus on man. This is "humanism." It is not to God or to goods that humans should assign most importance to, but to humans.

Well, what is so great about humans? For Marx it is our *creative power*:

If God has value, this God is *created*. That is, god does not create man, and man creates god.

If a work of art has value then that is because an artist *made* it. The creative activity conferred value to the creation. The value is not in the creation intrinsically. Actually the value is in the creative act or process.

If a product has value then that is because someone *manufactured* it. The banana was picked by someone, the house was built, etc.[2]

Marx's "creativism," as one might call it, is not only a doctrine about religions, emotional social relations, and art. It is also a theory of economics. One can distinguish between three theories of value in the history of economics:

(A) the *labor* theory,

(B) the *use* theory, and

(C) the *exchange* theory.

---

[1] *A Contribution to the Critique of Hegel's Philosophy of Right*, Introduction.
[2] How about creativism itself, is it a creation? Or does it lack value? The coherent answer is that it is not a creation and that it lacks value. Otherwise Marx would have to say that he creates the antropological phenomena he describes. He could not then say that he is right about society. He would be right, at most, about his own fiction. And of course he does not aim to be right about fiction. His object is society as it really is. But Marx does not seem to say this anywhere himself.

Marx is for (A), like many of the classic names of political economy before him, such as Adam Smith and David Ricardo. Contemporary economists tend to rely on (C). (B) is also a sensible alternative.

Here is a way to contrast (A)–(C). If your sculpture takes a lot of energy for you to produce then it has a high value by (A). But if the sculpture is of no use to anyone then it has a low value at (B). And if no one wants to buy it its value is low at (C) as well.

One needs to notice how rich the labor history of a final product can be, for instance in the case of a sculpture. What can add to the sculpture's labor value is your long training in art school, because the training was part of the labor that went into this sculpture. Also, if you go through many versions of a sculpture before you arrive at a product that you are satisfied with then the work that went into the earlier versions must added on to the final sum of energy that you consumed. It is not only the polishing of your best piece that has labor value. It is your entire history of training and preparing and overcoming shortcomings and obstacles.

We can also consider examples outside the arts. For example, diamonds have such a high value because it takes so much work to find them, and if we can get machines to do some of our work for us then the value of the products thus produced declines. On the other hand, the production of the machinery would then attain its own value. We will deal with the issue of machine production more amply in 4.2.

What is supposed to be so novel and surprising about Marx's creativism (as I am calling it)? Marx himself clearly believes that the analogy between capitalism and religion is especially revealing. They are irrational in a similar way:

> [...] the existence of the things *quâ* commodities, and the value relation between the products of labor which stamps them as commodities, have absolutely no connection with their physical properties and with the material relations arising therefrom. There it is a definite social relation between men, that assumes, in their eyes, the fantastic form of a relation between things. In order, therefore, to find an analogy, we must have recourse to the mist-enveloped regions of the religious world. In that world the productions of the human brain appear as independent beings endowed with life, and entering into relation both with one another and the human race.[1]

Again:

---

[1] *Capital*, I, Ch. I, 4.

the laborer exists to satisfy the needs of self-expansion of existing values, instead of, on the contrary, material wealth existing to satisfy the needs of development on the part of the laborer. As, in religion, man is governed by the products of his own brain, so in capitalistic production, he is governed by the products of his own hand.[1]

The analogy is constant. Modern capitalism is just like primitive animism. Why is this association supposed to be so important?

Everyone is familiar with the habit of young children to project personalities to inanimate objects. A young child can view a doll as a person, or even a tree. This same habit is found in many ancient religions, and scholars have called the habit "animism." For example, in many old religions there is a god in the sea, another in the sky (especially when it thunders), perhaps even in the fox and in the crow, etc. There seem to be few limitations to the projections of ancient humans and young children. They can see personalities and powers everywhere, because their powers of imagination are so great. But of course we consider *ourselves* civilized enough, or mature enough, to *not* be tricked by such illusions any longer. We are no longer children, and we know so much more than the ancient animists. We do not think of ourselves as fools. We tend rather to admit that projections are only projections, we feel, and we can be quite proud of this honesty. But as a dialectician Marx says that things are not as they seem. For, as before, dialectics can have counter-intuitive results that are nonetheless perfectly true. Hence, we should not pride ourselves on our maturity too soon. In modern societies we have *not* in general abolished animism. The same fiction lives on in our economies. We are like young children, and like primitive believers in nature gods, Marx is saying, whether we know it or not!

This is in effect to say that we are not immune to the turbulations of human history. Our time is not as new or mature as we may like to think. The age of the great discoveries is not past. There are still sweeping changes to come.

This point is so important that we need to dwell on it. Erich Fromm (a follower of Marx's who is associated with the Frankfurt School, on which see Appendix B) describes how Marxian alienation actually has a long history:

> The whole concept of alienation found its first expression in Western thought in the Old Testament concept of idolatry. The essence of what the prophets call "idolatry" is not that man worships many gods instead of only one. It is that the idols are the work of man's own hands — they are things, and man bows down

---

[1] *Capital*, Ch. XXIII, 1.

and worships things; worships that which he has created himself. In doing so he transforms himself into a thing. He transfers to the things of his creation the attributes of his own life, and instead of experiencing himself as the creating person, he is in touch with himself only by the worship of the idol. He has become estranged from his own life forces, from the wealth of his own potentialities, and is in touch with himself only in the indirect way of submission to life frozen in the idols. The deadness and emptiness of the idol is expressed in the Old Testament: "Eyes they have and they do not see, ears they have and they do not hear," etc. The more man transfers his own powers to the idols, the poorer he himself becomes, and the more dependent on the idols, so that they permit him to redeem a small part of what was originally his. The idols can be a godlike figure, the state, the church, a person, possessions.[1]

Idolatry is very widespread also in *contemporary* human life:

Idolatry changes its objects; it is by no means to be found only in those forms in which the idol has a so-called religious meaning. Idolatry is always the worship of something into which man has put his own creative powers, and to which he now submits, instead of experiencing himself in his creative act. Among the many forms of alienation, the most frequent one is alienation in language. If I express a feeling with a word, let us say, if I say "I love you," the word is meant to be an indication of the reality which exists within myself, the power of my loving. The word "love" is meant to be a symbol of the fact love, but as soon as it is spoken it tends to assume a life of its own, it becomes a reality. I am under the illusion that the saying of the word is the equivalent of the experience, and soon I say the word and feel nothing, except the thought of love which the word expresses. The alienation of language shows the whole complexity of alienation. Language is one of the most precious human achievements; to avoid alienation by not speaking would be foolish — yet one must be always aware of the danger of the spoken word, that it threatens to substitute itself for the living experience. The same holds true for all other achievements of man; ideas, art, any kind of man-made objects. They are man's creations; they are valuable aids for life, yet each one of them is also a trap, a temptation to confuse life with things, experience with artifacts, feeling with surrender and submission.[2]

This is to make human problems deep and wide. All speech, all writing, all concepts, and artworks, theories, technologies — all of these are "traps," in Fromm's language. Why? Because of Marx's reason. They are only aids (Fromm's term). They are aids for experience, feeling,

---

[1] From Chapter 5.
[2] From Chapter 5.

and real action. They are *only* aids. They are as such lifeless. But for some reason we human beings tend and over and again to value the lifeless aids as if they were something more. This is not a problem only for small children and ignorant primitives but for all humans, even for modern and mature adults. This is what Marx said above and it is also what Fromm is saying now. We humans, as tool-making animals, happen to be just a little bit too fascinated by the tools we make.

The question this begs is how this sweeping problem can possibly be solved. How can the reign of creation over creator end? How can human creativity progress from the fictions of idolatry and fetishism to conscious freedom and realistic self-expression? Marx explains:

> We pre-suppose labor in a form that stamps it as exclusively human. A spider conducts operations that resemble those of a weaver, and a bee puts to shame many an architect in the construction of her cells. But what distinguishes the worst architect from the best of bees is this, that the architect raises his structure in imagination before he erects it in reality. At the end of every labor-process, we get a result that already existed in the imagination of the laborer at its commencement. He not only effects a change of form in the material on which he works, but he also realizes a purpose of his own that gives the law to his modus operandi, and to which he must subordinate his will. And this subordination is no mere momentary act. Besides the exertion of the bodily organs, the process demands that, during the whole operation, the workman's will be steadily in consonance with his purpose. This means close attention.[1]

A spider acts on instinct in designing its web, just as a bird does in building its nest — and, one might add, just as an infant human normally does when she takes her first breath. None of this takes any conscious or intentional planning. But a grown human can deliberate and self-consciously make something she has not been determined to make by any gene, parent, or deity. In other words, mature humans are capable of freedom. This is the difference Marx has in mind. He draws the difference because he is for the conscious and free alternative and opposed to the instinctive. He wants us to make and create things, not simply to inherit them. We are not automatons. We are capable of attaining a higher mode of consciousness and activity.

Is this clear? If the sculptor can say of the completed sculpture that it is her creation then she attains self-consciousness. For then she can say: *I did that.* This sculpture reflects her *abilities* and *interests*, if she was given free rein to sculpt as she wanted and could (otherwise it is not evidence of her desires or abilities). Hence the sculpture works as a

---

[1] *Capital*, I, Ch. VII, 1.

kind of mirror. The sculptor sees herself from it. More exactly, she sees a reflection of some of her interests and abilities. She sees, for one thing, what she *can* do. For another thing, she can see what she *likes* to do. The sculpture is a kind of register of what she has inside. It shows what she really is, in terms of talents and desires.

The "mirror" now was a metaphor. Notice why a real mirror would not work for Marx. What you really are, for the creativist Marx, is someone capable of and interested in creative action. Your *drives* and *talents* are not visible in the mirror. Your drives are visible only from your efforts to live them out as fully as you can. In the mirror you see only a face. But the face does not show much about you. It shows someone dark or pale, young or old, hairy or not, etc. But none of that is an indication of any sort of personality inside. Dark does not right away mean smart, for example. Old does not imply calm, etc. You cannot know much about people based on their faces. They may sing well or badly: you do not know until you listen. They may sculpt, reason, joke, etc. You never know, based merely on their faces.

This is to say that the self-knower needs *external* objects. There must be something like clay to fashion or the self cannot be located. The sculptor's creative activity causes the clay to attain a shape and the product, as a sculpture, say of a nude human, has value. Until the sculpture is completed there is opposition, because the clay does not always behave in accordance with the sculptor's wishes. The clay resists the sculptor's pressures. It is an independent, external object. The sculptor must bend it to her will. The clay does not automatically adjust to the will of the sculpture. But, ironic as it is, the sculptor *needs just this resistance* in the external object to find her self-reflection at all! Otherwise she could not look at her creation as a thing that is independent from her own imagination. It must have its own character or it cannot be compared to. If you are to look in the mirror then the mirror must really be out there.

Consider, in contrast, what would happen if you attempted to find your self-image purely from your wishes. To see this, imagine that you had a mirror which changes exactly as you want it to. If you want to look handsome, it shows you as handsome, and if you want to seem scary it will show you something scary. Such a mirror would not give you any true feedback, of course. It would not show what you really look like. It would act like some kind of a prostitute or slave. It would obey your wishes but — for that very reason — it would not tell you anything about who you are. (This is dialectical thinking, of course.

There must be opposition or the self can never be revealed. If you lived in Disneyland then you could never find out who you are.)

In a similar way, Marx would not admit that you can identify your true self simply by meditating or introspecting. For no matter how you try to catch yourself in your thought-processes you do not actually produce anything that you can look at as an independent product. In meditating you would only be going in circles, always producing only what you think you produce. There would be no external sculpture to fasten on. The situation would be just as with the magic mirror which changes according to your wishes. What you need, to know yourself, is more than wishful thinking. This is a major point in Marx's dialectic.

The reader can probably guess that Marx is also very far from agreeing that anyone can actually identify their true selves by reference to what they *own*. If you are rich and buy a castle then that gives you no new characteristics as a personality. You are stuck with your old self inside the castle, no matter how glorious in decorum your castle is inside or outside. Things would be different, of course, if you *built* the castle, or if you at least *designed* it. But even then it would be the designing or building that would serve to express and identify your character, and it would not help you to *own* the castle at all. The completed castle would already refer to your past self, not to your present one. It would become a fetter if you clung to it. You always need to keep on creating. For Marx you would never get to relax and retire in the castle.

We have now seen that Marx celebrates human creativity. Each one of us is to do something we are good at. We need to realize our potentials. Does this mean that Marx subscribes to Plato's utopia, the Kallipolis? We can see why that appearance would arise. For the Platonic Kallipolis is indeed a city in which each agent realizes her potentials. In the Kallipolis the talented artisan gets to work as an artisan, the good singer must sing, etc. Similarly, for Marx a communist utopia is run by this rule: "From each according to his ability, to each according to his needs!"[1] Plato and Marx would seem to agree about this! Both are communists, and both want us to live by our talents.

But — and this is a large but — Marx does *not* want us to specialize, and in this he differs dramatically from Platonic as well as Hinduist thought. Marx says:

> He is a hunter, a fisherman, a herdsman, or a critical critic, and must remain so if he does not want to lose his means of livelihood; while in communist society, where nobody has one exclusive sphere of activity but each can become accomplished in any branch he

---

[1] From *Critique of the Gotha Program*, I.

wishes, society regulates the general production and thus makes it possible for me to do one thing today and another tomorrow, to hunt in the morning, fish in the afternoon, rear cattle in the evening, criticize after dinner, just as I have a mind, without ever becoming hunter, fisherman, herdsman or critic.[1]

Marx opposes the specialization of labor. He trusts that on an innate basis everyone is in fact many-sided in interests and in potentials (somewhat like the Renaissance man Leonardo da Vinci, who excels in art as well as science). No one is by nature suited only to a specialized task, Marx believes, be that of sweeping the streets or programming computers.

How does Marx claim to know that individuals have multiple talents and interests? He does not say that most individuals already say or think so. Marx's point is rather that in history humans have systematically behaved in this way, no matter what they have thought. What humans tend ordinarily to think or say is no reliable authority about what humans really can *do*. But it is normal for the truth to be surprising among humans:

> This seems paradox and contrary to every-day observation. It is also paradox that the earth moves round the sun, and that water consists of two highly inflammable gases. Scientific truth is always paradox, if judged by every-day experience, which catches only the delusive appearance of things.[2]

It is only to be expected, Marx is saying, that his results will sound strange. That is just what always happens when things are investigated rationally. Here Marx is following the ancient dialectical pathway which was trampled so much earlier by Zeno and Socrates. They, too, came upon strange results, and only by means of rational thought.

However, Marx's view that he is doing "science" needs to be taken with salt. He is not a physician or a chemist, obviously. He is a philosopher, a social theorist, and a historian. He thinks he can support his universalized ethic by a mass of historical facts, as he explains Ruge in a letter (from 1843):

> This does not mean that we shall confront the world with new doctrinaire principles and proclaim: Here is the truth, on your knees before it! It means that we shall develop for the world new principles from the existing principles of the world. We shall not say: Abandon your struggles, they are mere folly; let us provide you with true campaign-slogans. Instead, we shall simply show the world why

---

[1] From *German Ideology* Part 1, A.
[2] *Wages, Price, and Profit*, Ch. 6.

it is struggling, and consciousness of this is a thing it must acquire whether it wishes or not.

The reform of consciousness consists entirely in making the world aware of its own consciousness, in arousing it from its dream of itself, in explaining its own actions to it. Like Feuerbach's critique of religion, our whole aim can only be to translate religious and political problems into their self-conscious human form.

Our programme must be: the reform of consciousness not through dogmas but by analyzing mystical consciousness obscure to itself, whether it appear in religious or political form. It will then become plain that the world has long since dreamed of something of which it needs only to become conscious for it to possess it in reality. It will then become plain that our task is not to draw a sharp mental line between past and future, but to *complete* the thought of the past. Lastly, it will becomes plain that mankind will not begin any new work, but will consciously bring about the completion of its old work.

We are therefore in a position to sum up the credo of our journal in a *single word*: the self-clarification (critical philosophy) of the struggles and wishes of the age. This is a task for the world and for us. It can succeed only as the product of united efforts. What is needed above all is a *confession*, and nothing more than that. To obtain forgiveness for its sins, mankind needs only to declare them for what they are.

Marx does not wish to command individuals to obey the values he has portrayed. He wants rather to show that the values have been theirs all along. In Kant's terms, Marx is not doing ethics. He is closer to anthropology. He is for whatever values all humans already are for. So he does not want to *change* values. On the other hand, Marx holds, as we have already seen, that the real values of many individuals are actually *concealed*. Their values are often concealed from themselves. Only in the communist utopia would they finally come out with their real characters and interests, Marx says.

That is the story so far.

4.2 The Materialistic Dialectic

But Marx is also a *materialist*. What is materialism? Marx himself says:

The first premise of all human history is, of course, the existence of living human individuals. Thus the first fact to be established is the physical organization of these individuals and their consequent relation to the rest of nature. Of course, we cannot here go either into the actual physical nature of man, or into the natural conditions in which man finds himself — geological, hydrographical, climatic and so on. The writing of history must always set out from these natural bases and their modification in the course of history through the action of men.

Men can be distinguished from animals by consciousness, by religion or anything else you like. They themselves begin to distinguish themselves from animals as soon as they begin to produce their means of subsistence, a step which is conditioned by their physical organization. By producing their means of subsistence men are indirectly producing their actual material life.

The way in which men produce their means of subsistence depends first of all on the nature of the actual means of subsistence they find in existence and have to reproduce. This mode of production must not be considered simply as being the production of the physical existence of the individuals. Rather it is a definite form of activity of these individuals, a definite form of expressing their life, a definite mode of life on their part. As individuals express their life, so they are. What they are, therefore, coincides with their production, both with what they produce and with how they produce. The nature of individuals thus depends on the material conditions determining their production.[1]

This is the *materialistic* dialectic in Marx. The self-creative agent is a tool-maker. She lifts herself in the air by the hair, as it were, in that she not only *uses* certain tools that she is given but actually *makes* them. So she herself lifts herself above the level of fate. She makes more things possible than the givens of reality offer to her. She seizes power.

The great human transition from a passive role in history to an active role is made vivid in the ancient Greek myth of Prometheus, which is narrated in Aeschylus' play *Prometheus Bound*. Prometheus steals fire from the gods. The ability to make fire is an ability to fashion tools. It leads to the ability to melt metals. So it does not lead only to the deliberate control of heat and light per se. It is a tool for tools! The same play speaks also of the introduction of the alphabet and of numbers in connection to Prometheus' act. These, too, are types of second-order tool: tools for more tools. For with letters and numbers all kinds of generative possibilities are opened up, from literary traditions to orderly structures of argument, proofs, geometries, astronomies, calculi, even computer programs (and whatever else may lie in our future). Innovations like fire-making and alphabets and numbers enable so many further innovations. They are "meta" tools, one might say.

[1] Ibid.

But this about meta-tools is not only ancient history. For also in modern life the real materialistic transitions are systematically due to novel developments in technology. The major technological innovation in the industrial period in which Marx lived was perhaps the steam engine, by James Watt in 1751. Marx explains its background thus:

> Of all the great motors handed down from the manufacturing period, horse-power is the worst, partly because a horse has a head of his own, partly because he is costly, and the extent to which he is applicable in factories is very restricted. Nevertheless the horse was extensively used during the infancy of modern industry. [...]But for all that, the use of water, as the predominant motive power, was beset with difficulties. It could not be increased at will, it failed at certain seasons of the year, and, above all, it was essentially local. Not till the invention of Watt's second and so-called double-acting steam-engine, was a prime mover found, that begot its own force by the consumption of coal and water, whose power was entirely under man's control, that was mobile and a means of locomotion [...]. The greatness of Watt's genius showed itself in the specification of the patent that he took out in April, 1784. In that specification his steam-engine is described, not as an invention for a specific purpose, but as an agent universally applicable in Mechanical Industry.[1]

The horse did not always *obey* its owner. Water, again, was available as a source of power only in *some* places. In contrast, the steam engine was reliable and movable. What is more, it could be used to produce very many kinds of thing, so it seemed "universally applicable." Still more, the steam engine could eventually be used to produce parts for copies of *itself*, so it could be used as a kind of super-machine that reproduced itself:

> [...] apart from the radical changes introduced in the construction of sailing vessels, the means of communication and transport became gradually adapted to the modes of production of mechanical industry, by the creation of a system of river steamers, railways, ocean steamers, and telegraphs. But the huge masses of iron that had now to be forged, to be welded, to be cut, to be bored, and to be shaped, demanded, on their part, cyclopean machines, for the construction of which the methods of the manufacturing period were utterly inadequate. Modern industry had therefore itself to take in hand the machine, its characteristic instrument of production, and to construct machines by machines. It was not till it did this, that it built up for itself a fitting technical foundation, and stood on its own feet. Machinery, simultaneously with the increasing use of it, in the first decades of this century, appropriated, by degrees, the fabrication of machines

---

[1] *Capital*, I, Ch. XV, 1.

proper. But it was only during the decade preceding 1866, that the construction of railways and ocean steamers on a stupendous scale called into existence the cyclopean machines now employed in the construction of prime movers.[1]

This kind of an image is vital to Marx's materialistic dialectic. He needs material life to have a dialectical structure if he is to analyze modern, industrial life by means of dialectical tools. He finds this structure, ultimately, in the metallic "prime mover" of the Industrial Age. The "prime mover," or in other words the first mover, the unmoved mover, or the self-mover, is in Plato's and Aristotle's philosophies *God*. This is the place that Marx's super-machine is now supposed to occupy. This is the level on which Marx wants his dialectic to operate.

Marx's picture can look dystopian and totalitarian, recalling George Orwell's *Nineteen Eighty-Four* with its robotic controls over human individuals. But this is not the kind of thing that is on Marx's mind. Marx would point out that *humans* ultimately produce all the machines, even the engine-making engine. The super-engine does not come and find us. We make it, in history. Moreover, the laboring machines are there only for a human purpose. Hence, at both ends, that is at the origins and at the purposes, we find humans. The machines are confined to the middle. They do not invent and they can never become purposes of their own.

But we need at this point also to understand, on a rather general level, how Marx works with two very different dialectics. One of his dialectics is humanistic, and we surveyed that in 4.1. His other dialectic is materialistic, and we have been concerned with it in this section, 4.2. We must be careful to notice how different these two dialectics are. For there are deep reasons why human roles cannot be exchanged between the two dialectics. Obviously, art, love, and criticism cannot take over as materialistic tools. They do not change the material order. They are mere symbols and emotions, and they are materially powerless and useless. Materially they make very little difference in the world. On the other side, Watt's steam engine makes a great material difference in the world, vastly increasing human powers to meddle with the material environment. But Watt's invention of the steam engine is, for its part, hardly a self-expressive act in humanistic terms. It is a smart invention, and it is very useful, but it would be nonsense to say that it expresses Watt's *personality* or that Watt realizes *all his potentials* in making the machine. So we need to keep the different dialectics apart inside Marx. Both of the dialectics are self-corrective in structure, and that is

---

[1] Ibid.

why they both qualify as dialectics in the first place. They are "prime movers." But only one is humanistic and properly self-expressive and only one is materialistic. Much trouble results if one confuses the two (as we will see soon below, in 4.3).

Yet Marx does not introduce the two dialectics only to keep them apart. He believes they work together. How? He answers:

> In fact, the realm of freedom actually begins only where labor which is determined by necessity and mundane considerations ceases; thus in the very nature of things it lies beyond the sphere of actual material production. Just as the savage must wrestle with Nature to satisfy his wants, to maintain and reproduce life, so must civilized man, and he must do so in all social formations and under all possible modes of production. With his development this realm of physical necessity expands as a result of his wants; but, at the same time, the forces of production which satisfy these wants also increase. Freedom in this field can only consist in socialized man, the associated producers, rationally regulating their interchange with Nature, bringing it under their common control, instead of being ruled by it as by the blind forces of Nature; and achieving this with the least expenditure of energy and under conditions most favorable to, and worthy of, their human nature. But it nonetheless still remains a realm of necessity. Beyond it begins that development of human energy which is an end in itself, the true realm of freedom, which, however, can blossom forth only with this realm of necessity as its basis. The shortening of the working-day is its basic prerequisite.[1]

This message can hardly be expressed more clearly. Freedom begins where necessity ends. Necessity is material. Humans need to get organized materially first and after this they can be mentally free. In other words, in history one needs to work through a materialistic dialectic before one can enjoy a humanistic dialectic. The phase of materialistic organization is for Marx a mere prelude or pre-history, and the actual events of real human history belong to the future, to the humanistic side.

Does this mean that Marx is a totalitarian after all, namely in thinking that our mental and cultural freedoms must wait until the communist revolution has been conducted? Is he saying that we need to sacrifice our familiar freedoms, like the freedom to think or speak as we happen to please, or the freedom to publish and to congregate as we like, merely so that we can serve the project of completing the super-machine, like ants? No. For notice that Marx is not saying that everyone should serve the super-machine first and only later get their familiar freedoms. He

---

[1] *Capital*, III, Ch. XLVIII, 3.

is not saying that we need now to learn to sacrifice the rights we are accustomed to enjoying under liberal constitutions, and that after a period of material service we will finally get our liberal rights back. This is not his message. He is saying, rather, that we *are already in fact* serving the big machine all the time, and that this will continue to be so until the materially based utopia will come. The liberal rights that so often get advertised in Western societies are not rights of the truly free. We are *not* familiar with true freedom. Freedom is something more radical than what we are accustomed to as citizens of liberal societies.

How can this be? How is it possible that our intuitions about freedom are so mistaken? On one level, we may be unused to considering how we live by fetishism or idolatry, and this story was already told in the previous section (4.1). So we may tend to think, as we are often told to think in liberal societies, that we are free if only we can vote in elections, speak up in public, own property, etc. To us, self-expression can sound like an exotic goal. Its concrete meaning may seem far-fetched and elusive. But nonetheless it amounts to true freedom, Marx says. But on a further, materialistic level the story continues. For Marx holds that there are underlying material causes for our illusions. The center of the materialistic problem for him is that in history we do not normally find that humans control materials at all. What happens mostly in history is that the materials control *them*:

> In history up to the present it is certainly an empirical fact that separate individuals have, with the broadening of their activity into world-historical activity, become more and more enslaved under a power alien to them (a pressure which they have conceived of as a dirty trick on the part of the so-called universal spirit, etc.), a power which has become more and more enormous and, in the last instance, turns out to be the world market. But it is just as empirically established that, by the overthrow of the existing state of society by the communist revolution (of which more below) and the abolition of private property which is identical with it, this power, which so baffles the German theoreticians, will be dissolved; and that then the liberation of each single individual will be accomplished in the measure in which history becomes transformed into world history. From the above it is clear that the real intellectual wealth of the individual depends entirely on the wealth of his real connections. Only then will the separate individuals be liberated from the various national and local barriers, be brought into practical connection with the material and intellectual production of the whole world and be put in a position to acquire the capacity to enjoy this all-sided production of the whole earth (the creations of man). All-round dependence, this natural form of the world-historical co-operation of individuals, will be transformed by this communist revolution

into the control and conscious mastery of these powers, which, born of the action of men on one another, have till now overawed and governed men as powers completely alien to them.[1]

Marx argues that communism will unleash so much energy. Undreamt of purposes will arise. This is on a par with his materialistic belief that matter rules minds. If you change the material order in a society then new thoughts and emotions are bound to arise. But it follows from this same materialism that we cannot yet so much as imagine what will happen mentally in a communist utopia. For we are all tied down to the current material order. We cannot see ahead.

There is a certain egalitarianism in Marx's view that all of us suffer from the drawbacks of the reigning material order. But he does not at all hold that we suffer equally. There are different *classes*.

How do they arise? As soon as new tools for work have been introduced in history, divisions of labor have soon been enforced on their basis. For there has always been a class owning the tools and then another class doing the actual work of using those tools in everyday labor. This seems to have been so in every society as soon as recognizable societies were first formed in the Neolithic Revolution, starting about 10 000 years ago. This is when humans gradually turned from hunting and gathering to farming, and this is when they started to stay in certain regions instead of wandering around. This is also when they built the first towns, and — because farming did not require the labor of everyone — specialized professions were born. Some farmed, some worked in crafts, some were warriors or guardians, and in very many places there was also a religious elite which did not work. Writing emerged, mathematical regularities were revealed, etc. We know of similar patterns in the same period from Southwest Asia, India, China, and Meso-America.

The generalization that Marx makes about classes in ancient times is that then slaves did the work for slave-owners. For instance, in Periclean Athens, at the time of the greatest cultural glory of that city, there were, according to some estimates, around 40 000 free citizens and up to 300 000 slaves. The free minority were free to go to the theater, debate philosophy, sculpt, dance, etc. The less free majority were held back from such activities by *material realities*. Later, in the European medieval period, landowners owned the land and serfs worked it. Again the landowners were the minority. And what compelled the serfs to work? Material reality. They needed food and clothes and shelter. (Who do you think controlled the armies and castles?) And again,

---

[1] From *German Ideology* Part 1, A.

predictably, in the Industrial Age, we find factory-owning capitalists on the one side and the factory-working majority on the other. In this period it is normal, in many countries, for the judicial systems to invoke individual rights. But these are not rights to food, say, or to shoes. They are rights to express one's views in public, to practice whatever religion one likes, etc. They are not rights to schooling or medical care. There were no public libraries. The "rights" were only rhetorical, Marx says. You were *allowed*, by law, to do many things that you were not physically *able* to do, so the rights were pretty meaningless to the poor majority. (Similarly, you are allowed, now, to fly. Why don't you do it? No one is stopping you! Just beat your wings!)

One might ask, at this juncture, whether Marx does not actually have a *dialectic* of social classes? Is the conflict between workers and capitalists, or between peasants and feudal lords, or between slaves and slave-owners, not dialectical? It is not entirely. The reason is that the class conflicts of Marxian history are always based on something more fundamental: productive relations. If new productive tools are introduced then this has social effects, as an old elite has to go and a new one takes its place. (For example, once factory production originated and spread in England the old land-owning class lost much of its power. The new middle class then created its own rhetoric of individual rights, which came to be inscribed later in so many liberal constitutions — that is, *after* the middle class had already taken power in material terms. The "right" is always recognized only after the "might": that is materialism.) The social formations are only a kind of surface layer that flutters above the harder and deeper material facts. Class conflicts could not possibly result in innovations on their own, so they are not self-movers or dialectical agents. Classes belong only to the fluttering surface.[1]

In sum, there is in Marx a mental dialectic and a material one. The mental is free and the material is only organizational. The material has to come before the mental, Marx says.

Now let us see where some of Marx's leading followers have taken these ideas. It will be evident quite quickly that they have bent him out of shape.

---

1 In *The Poverty of Philosophy*, Chapter 2, Marx writes: "In acquiring new productive forces men change their mode of production; and in changing their mode of production, in changing the way of earning their living, they change all their social relations. The hand-mill gives you society with the feudal lord; the steam-mill society with the industrial capitalist."

4.3 The "Marxists"

Engels begins to speak for many communists and socialists after Marx's death. He has in many ways seemed to readers to be more sober than Marx, though also less of a genius. Engels is a kind of Dr. Watson, if Marx is Sherlock Holmes.

All of the following excerpts are from Engels' *Anti-Dühring*, published in 1878:

> Dialectics [...] is nothing more than the science of the general laws of motion and development of nature, human society and thought.

The central element in dialectics, says Engels, is the negation of the negation.

> And so, what is the negation of the negation? An extremely general — and for this reason extremely far-reaching and important — law of development of nature, history, and thought; a law which, as we have seen, holds good in the animal and plant kingdoms, in geology, in mathematics, in history and in philosophy [...].

We see that for Engels dialectics apply very widely. Well, what are they? One needs to look at things in motion, Engels says:

> True, so long as we consider things as at rest and lifeless, each one by itself, alongside and after each other, we do not run up against any contradictions in them. We find certain qualities which are partly common to, partly different from, and even contradictory to each other, but which in the last-mentioned case are distributed among different objects and therefore contain no contradiction within. Inside the limits of this sphere of observation we can get along on the basis of the usual, metaphysical mode of thought. But the position is quite different as soon as we consider things in their motion, their change, their life, their reciprocal influence on one another. Then we immediately become involved in contradictions. Motion itself is a contradiction: even simple mechanical change of position can only come about through a body being at one and the same moment of time both in one place and in another place, being in one and the same place and also not in it. And the continuous origination and simultaneous solution of this contradiction is precisely what motion is.

This brings to mind Zeno, from Chapter 1. One of his paradoxes was that of the Arrow. The arrow is and is not in one place at each instant. Engels seems to be agreeing with Zeno. (But recall that we did not agree with Zeno. We said that there do not need to be atomic instants of motion any more than there need to be individual musical notes which contain whole melodies. One cannot reduce all things to their smallest parts.) Here are Engels' examples:

Let us take a grain of barley. Billions of such grains of barley are milled, boiled and brewed and then consumed. But if such a grain of barley meets with conditions which are normal for it, if it falls on suitable soil, then under the influence of heat and moisture it undergoes a specific change, it germinates; the grain as such ceases to exist, it is negated, and in its place appears the plant which has arisen from it, the negation of the grain. But what is the normal life-process of this plant? It grows, flowers, is fertilized and finally once more produces grains of barley, and as soon as these have ripened the stalk dies, is in its turn negated. As a result of this negation of the negation we have once again the original grain of barley, but not as a single unit, but ten-, twenty- or thirtyfold. Species of grain change extremely slowly, and so the barley of today is almost the same as it was a century ago. But if we take a plastic ornamental plant, for example a dahlia or an orchid, and treat the seed and the plant which grows from it according to the gardener's art, we get as a result of this negation of the negation not only more seeds, but also qualitatively improved seeds, which produce more beautiful flowers, and each repetition of this process, each fresh negation of the negation, enhances this process of perfection. — With most insects, this process follows the same lines as in the case of the grain of barley. Butterflies, for example, spring from the egg by a negation of the egg, pass through certain transformations until they reach sexual maturity, pair and are in turn negated, dying as soon as the pairing process has been completed and the female has laid its numerous eggs. We are not concerned at the moment with the fact that with other plants and animals the process does not take such a simple form, that before they die they produce seeds, eggs or offspring not once but many times; our purpose here is only to show that the negation of the negation *really does take place* in both kingdoms of the organic world. Furthermore, the whole of geology is a series of negated negations, a series of successive chatterings of old and deposits of new rock formations. First the original earth crust brought into existence by the cooling of the liquid mass was broken up by oceanic, meteorological and atmospherico-chemical action, and these fragmented masses were stratified on the ocean bed. Local upheavals of the ocean bed above the surface of the sea subject portions of these first strata once more to the action of rain, the changing temperature of the seasons and the oxygen and carbonic acid of the atmosphere. These same influences act on the molten masses of rock which issue from the interior of the earth, break through the strata and subsequently cool off. In this way, in the course of millions of centuries, ever new strata are formed and in turn are for the most part destroyed, ever anew serving as material for the formation of new strata. But the result of this process has been a very positive one: the creation of a soil composed of the most varied chemical elements and mechanically fragmented, which makes possible the most abundant and diversified vegetation.

I think anyone can understand what Engels is *trying* to say. Every change is a negation, and a series of changes is a series of negations. Several changes or negations result in an ascent, of some sort, to a higher kind of life.[1]

But does this make good sense? What is vague in it is that now "negation" stands for so many different kinds of change. It is "negation" for a seed to grow, for rain to fall, etc. If all change can simply be *called* "negation" then there is no advantage to introducing the new word, "negation," and one might as well use only "change." And then nothing would follow for dialectics. Dialectics would be only air.

But how does Engels see this? He notices the problem:

> But someone may object: the negation that has taken place in this case is not a real negation: I negate a grain of barley also when I grind it, an insect when I crush it underfoot, or the positive quantity *a* when I cancel it, and so on. Or I negate the sentence: the rose is a rose, when I say: the rose is not a rose; and what do I get if I then negate this negation and say: but after all the rose is a rose? — These objections are in fact the chief arguments put forward by the metaphysicians against dialectics, and they are wholly worthy of the narrow-mindedness of this mode of thought. Negation in dialectics does not mean simply saying no, or declaring that something does not exist, or destroying it in any way one likes. Long ago Spinoza said: *Omnis determinatio est negatio* — every limitation or determination is at the same time a negation. And further: the kind of negation is here determined, firstly, by the general and, secondly, by the particular nature of the process. I must not only negate, but also sublate the negation. I must therefore so arrange the first negation that the second remains or becomes possible. How? This depends on the particular nature of each individual case. If I grind a grain of barley, or crush an insect, I have carried out the first part of the action, but have made the second part impossible. Every kind of thing therefore has a peculiar way of being negated in such manner that it gives rise to a development, and it is just the same with every kind of conception or idea. The infinitesimal calculus involves a form of negation which is different from that used in the formation of positive powers from

---

[1] There is also another famous concern in Hegelian dialectics, how changes in quantity, when great enough, become changes in quality. Engels discusses this as well. I exclude it because "dialectics" with an aspect like this is not something Plato or Kant would share. It is a specifically Hegelian element which this book's larger discussion does not need.

negative roots. This has to be learnt, like everything else. The bare knowledge that the barley plant and the infinitesimal calculus are both governed by negation of negation does not enable me either to grow barley successfully or to differentiate and integrate; just as little as the bare knowledge of the laws of the determination of sound by the dimensions of the strings enables me to play the violin.

What is unhelpful in this passage is, again, the reference to individual variations. For if negation will be different in every case then it is hard to see what the cases have in common, and then the general meaning of dialectic (or Engelsian dialectic) is lost.

More helpful is the reference to playing violin. Knowing *about* playing the violin is not yet knowing how to actually *play*. The theory of music is not music. Engels must mean that the player grasps, or performs, the negations, while the theoretician of violins does not really understand. So one performs the negations or one does not really "get" them. But even this is not *very* helpful. One can still doubt that in Engels' mouth "negation" means anything at all. For what does the barley seed *do*? It is only a seed. Things happen to it but it performs no actions. Moreover, the empirical events involving its growth are complex; so are all of the smallest changes small negations? If yes you get millions of negations per second. But we cannot live through all the changes of barley seeds; only barley seeds can, and we are not barley seeds. Engels' dialectic comes very close to being nonsense.

But we should ask: When can one *not* doubt the power of negation in a similar fashion? The answer is: In cases like Socrates', Kant's, and Marx's. Socrates offers paradoxes and engages in self-criticism and formalizes self-relations. Kant describes cosmological antinomies and ethical self-overcomings. Marx explains self-revision in creative acts and material production. These dialectics are not questionable in the way that Engels' are. Why? What is the big difference? Well, the real dialectics are all made of things *human*. We identify negations with contradictions in language or between incompatible desires, for example. It is too far from here to barley seeds. Things we *make* are dialectical. The machinery we use can be dialectical, but already spiders weaving their webs cannot.

How can a learned man like Engels work with dialectics if his conception of dialectics is this mistaken? How can he believe dialectics to make any real difference? The fact is, actually, that he does *not* hold that dialectics have great causal potentials. His real motive seems to be to try to save Marx's reputation.

[...] Marx does not intend to prove that the process was historically necessary. On the contrary: only after he has proved from history that in fact the process has partially already occurred, and partially must occur in the future, he in addition characterizes it as a process which develops in accordance with a definite dialectical law. That is all. It is therefore once again a pure distortion of the facts by Herr Dühring when he declares that the negation of the negation has to serve here as the midwife to deliver the future from the womb of the past, or that Marx wants anyone to be convinced of the necessity of the common ownership of land and capital (which is itself a Dühringian contradiction in corporeal form) on the basis of credence in the negation of the negation.

Engels is saying that dialectic cannot be used to generate new ages from older ones. Dialectic is *not* the motor of history. Rather, we are to find out what the facts of history are quite independently of dialectic and then we can find, separately, that the facts happen to accord with dialectics or that they do not. That is *all*. Dialectic has no grand role in Engels' research project. It is just a little bit of decoration that can be sprinkled on top of the real cake. Engels is mainly interested in finding out the empirical facts. Dialectic comes second. And is this what Marx said? By no means. In Marx dialectic is the motor but you find the motor working only in creative activities and not in nature (e.g. spiders, barley). So Engels just takes things in his own direction. He is not a Marxist. If you will, he wipes off the *human* face of Marxism and dialectics.

We see this especially well if we consider what Engels says about freedom:

Hegel was the first to state correctly the relation between freedom and necessity. To him, freedom is the insight into necessity (*die Einsicht in die Notwendigkeit*). "Necessity is *blind* only *in so far as it is not understood* [begriffen]." Freedom does not consist in any dreamt-of independence from natural laws, but in the knowledge of these laws, and in the possibility this gives of systematically making them work towards definite ends. This holds good in relation both to the laws of external nature and to those which govern the bodily and mental existence of men themselves — two classes of laws which we can separate from each other at most only in thought but not in reality. Freedom of the will therefore means nothing but the capacity to make decisions with knowledge of the subject. Therefore the *freer* a man's judgment is in relation to a definite question, the greater is the *necessity* with which the content of this judgment will be determined; while the uncertainty, founded on ignorance, which seems to make an arbitrary choice among many different and conflicting possible decisions, shows precisely by this that it is not free, that it is controlled by the very object it should itself control. Freedom therefore consists in the control over ourselves and over external nature, a control founded on knowledge of natural necessity; it is therefore necessarily a product of historical development. The first men who separated themselves from the animal kingdom were in all essentials as unfree as the animals themselves, but each step forward in the field of culture was a step towards freedom. On the threshold of human history stands the discovery that mechanical motion can be transformed into heat: the production of fire by friction; at the close of the development so far gone through stands the discovery that heat can be transformed into mechanical motion: the steam-engine. — And, in spite of the gigantic liberating revolution in the social world which the steam-engine is carrying through, and which is not yet half completed, it is beyond all doubt that the generation of fire by friction has had an even greater effect on the liberation of mankind. For the generation of fire by friction gave man for the first time control over one of the forces of nature, and thereby separated him forever from the animal kingdom. The steam-engine will never bring about such a mighty leap forward in human development, however important it may seem in our eyes as representing all those immense productive forces dependent on it — forces which alone make possible a state of society in which there are no longer class distinctions or anxiety over the means of subsistence for the individual, and in which for the first time there can be talk of real human freedom, of an existence in harmony with the laws of nature that have become known. But how young the whole of human history still is, and how ridiculous it would be to attempt to ascribe any absolute validity to our present views, is evident from the simple fact that all past history can be characterized as the history of the epoch from the practical discovery of the transformation of mechanical motion into heat up to that of the transformation of heat into mechanical motion.

Liberty for Engels is only about knowing what one has to do.[1] It is about engineers finding the way forwards to material progress. It

---

[1] He gives the credits to *Hegel*, the reader sees. One should be careful about this because Hegel can be interpreted variously. There is also a very different Hegel of the "young" or "left" Hegelians whom the early Marx also seems to cherish. In recent philosophy Adorno and Marcuse have made use of this aspect of Hegel; see Appendix B below. Engels, or an Engelsian, could insist that he is right about the *mature* Hegel, whose view is more thoroughly considered and less sketchy. But this would be like insisting that *Plato's* later dialogues must be better than his earlier ones. It is something one can argue for but it is not something obvious. The old are not always wiser than the young. I am not saying that youth is always better, but I *would* argue that the

has nothing to do with humanistic self-expression, self-predication, midwifery, gods, antinomies, or contra-causal wills. Engels' world is a kind of robot-universe in which the material facts dictate everything. They obey no higher laws. And all minds and wills and cultural artifacts must find their way to conform to the same. All deviations are childish illusions. Everyone must obey the super-machine. There is nothing else.

Soon we will see whether some great figures of real-world socialism followed Engels: Lenin and Mao. But before them, let us go into Bernstein's revisionism.

Bernstein. When Marx's predictions about history started to run into trouble his followers faced a choice whether to follow him further or not. For example, Marx had predicted that the rate of profits would steadily decline as capitalism advances, and that pay-levels would decline to a minimum and capitalists would be fewer and fewer. There would be more poor and less rich. But history took a different course, and at least in Western countries one started to see more rich individuals. Hence Marx was disproved. The issue that arose at that point was whether Marx was *utterly* disproved. Something he said was wrong — but was it *all* wrong? No, said Eduard Bernstein in his *Evolutionary Socialism*, in the year 1907. Marx is part wrong, not all wrong:

> For the general sympathy with the strivings for emancipation of the working classes does not in itself stand in the way of the scientific method. But, as Marx approaches a point when that final aim enters seriously into the question, he becomes uncertain and unreliable. Such contradictions then appear as were shown in the book under consideration, for instance, in the section on the movement of incomes in modern society. It thus appears that this great scientific spirit was, in the end, a slave to a doctrine. To express it figuratively, he has raised a mighty building within the framework of a scaffolding he found existing, and in its erection he kept strictly to the laws of scientific architecture as long as they did not collide with the conditions which the construction of the scaffolding prescribed, but he neglected or evaded them when the scaffolding did not allow of their observance. Where the scaffolding put limits in the way of the building, instead of destroying the scaffolding, he changed the building itself at the cost of its right proportions and so made it all the more dependent on the scaffolding. Was it the consciousness of this irrational relation which caused him continually to pass from

---

younger Hegel is a better dialectician than the older one and that the younger Plato, too, is a clear notch above the mature man. Vast lists of names and sources could be invoked on both sides of these debates, however! I do not pretend to have refuted Engels about Hegel by means of these small notes.

completing his work to amending special parts of it? However that may be, my conviction is that wherever that dualism shows itself the scaffolding must fall if the building is to grow in its right proportions. In the latter, and not in the former, is found what is worthy to live in Marx.

Nothing confirms me more in this conception than the anxiety with which some persons seek to maintain certain statements in *Capital*, which are falsified by facts. It is just some of the more deeply devoted followers of Marx who have not been able to separate themselves from the dialectical form of the work — that is the scaffolding alluded to — who do this. At least, that is only how I can explain the words of a man, otherwise so amenable to facts as Kautsky, who, when I observed in Stuttgart that the number of wealthy people for many years had increased, not decreased, answered: "If that were true then the date of our victory would not only be very long postponed, but we should never attain our goal. If it be capitalists who increase and not those with no possessions, then we are going ever further from our goal the more evolution progresses, theft capitalism grows stronger, not socialism."

That the number of the wealthy increases and does not diminish is not an invention of bourgeois "harmony economists," but a fact established by the boards of assessment for taxes, often to the chagrin of those concerned, a fact which can no longer be disputed. But what is the significance of this fact as regards the victory of socialism? Why should the realization of socialism depend on its refutation? Well, simply for this reason: because the dialectical scheme seems so to prescribe it; because a post threatens to fall out of the scaffolding if one admits that the social surplus product is appropriated by an increasing instead of a decreasing number of possessors. But it is only the speculative theory that is affected by this matter; it does not at all affect the actual movement. Neither the struggle of the workers for democracy in politics nor their struggle for democracy in industry is touched by it. The prospects of this struggle do not depend on the theory of concentration of capital in the hands of a diminishing number of magnates, nor on the whole dialectical scaffolding of which this is a plank, but on the growth of social wealth and of the social productive forces, in conjunction with general social progress, and, particularly, in conjunction with the intellectual and moral advance of the working classes themselves.

For Bernstein, Marx is like a master builder. He has a "scaffolding" which helps him build some things but which also holds back his building ability sometimes. This scaffolding, metaphorically, is dialectical. Now Bernstein says that the building process should not stop even if the scaffolding gets in the way. One should get *rid* of the scaffolding if it proves detrimental. The socialistic construction should go on regardless. In other words, dialectic is not at the heart of socialism. If dialectic dies, socialism can still go on living. That is Bernstein's message.

Bernstein was the most vocal person to express this view, but several others acted on views like his without preaching them as loudly in public. Karl Kautsky is perhaps the individual with the greatest influence among reformist socialists in the late nineteenth and early twentieth centuries. He practiced reformism while not preaching it, advocating, in practice, a platform of moderate reforms: a shorter working day, children's rights, women's rights, universal education, universal health care, etc. Kautsky was followed by social democrats across Northern Europe who created the so-called "welfare state," which is in many respects a living reality to this day.[1]

In this context one should notice the effect of the issue about dialectics on politics. Bernsteinian "revisionism" was for gradual reforms, not for revolutions. Dialectics are revolutionary, and Bernstein wanted to get rid of the false historical laws of Marxian dialectics. We need gradual reforms; we need to slow down, Bernstein said. This meant *not* upsetting the liberal democratic system. It meant participating in elections and endorsing the political system of liberal democracy. It also meant the acceptance of private ownership and big business. One needed to tax business to fund the social projects. But one would not abolish business, or collectivize private property. This is in sharp contrast with what Marx himself says, so there is indeed a "revision." The great contradictions and the self-movers disappear in Bernstein, and socialism becomes a mere extension of liberal democracy.

Lenin's response to Marx's mistaken prediction is different. He does not sacrifice dialectics like Bernstein, so he remains radical. The same "scaffolding" can stay. But still the construction itself changes its shape remarkably.

Lenin says (in his "One Step Forward, Two Steps Back" in the year 1904):

> ...the great Hegelian dialectics which Marxism made its own, having first turned it right side up, must never be confused with the vulgar trick of justifying the zigzags of politicians who swing over from the revolutionary to the opportunist wing of the Party, with the vulgar habit of lumping together particular statements, and particular developmental factors, belonging to different stages

---

[1] Kautsky does not attack dialectic like Bernstein does. But nonetheless Kautsky is in practice a reformist rather than a revolutionary. On this see Sassoon Chapter 1.

of a single process. Genuine dialectics does not justify the errors of individuals, but studies the inevitable turns, proving that they were inevitable by a detailed study of the process of development in all its concreteness. [...]

One step forward, two steps back.... It happens in the lives of individuals, and it happens in the history of nations and in the development of parties. It would be the most criminal cowardice to doubt even for a moment the inevitable and complete triumph of the principles of revolutionary Social-Democracy, of proletarian organization and Party discipline. We have already won a great deal, and we must go on fighting, undismayed by reverses, fighting steadfastly, scorning the philistine methods of circle wrangling, doing our very utmost to preserve the hard-won single Party tie linking all Russian Social-Democrats, and striving by dint of persistent and systematic work to give all Party members, and the workers in particular, a full and conscious understanding of the duties of Party members, of the struggle at the Second Party Congress, of all the causes and all the stages of our divergence, and of the utter disastrousness of opportunism, which, in the sphere of organization as in the sphere of our programmed and our tactics, helplessly surrenders to the bourgeois psychology, uncritically adopts the point of view of bourgeois democracy, and blunts the weapon of the class struggle of the proletariat.

In its struggle for power the proletariat has no other weapon but organization. Disunited by the rule of anarchic competition in the bourgeois world, ground down by forced labor for capital, constantly thrust back to the "lower depths" of utter destitution, savagery, and degeneration, the proletariat can, and inevitably will, become an invincible force only through its ideological unification on the principles of Marxism being reinforced by the material unity of organization, which welds millions of toilers into an army of the working class. Neither the senile rule of the Russian autocracy nor the senescent rule of international capital will be able to withstand this army. It will more and more firmly close its ranks, in spite of all zigzags and backward steps, in spite of the opportunist phrase-mongering of the Girondists of present-day Social-Democracy, in spite of the self-satisfied exaltation of the retrograde circle spirit, and in spite of the tinsel and fuss of intellectualist anarchism.

Lenin is saying that the true representatives of dialectic do not try to justify flimsy experiments or arbitrary contradictions, because what is dialectical is really only what proves to be necessary as a real force in the long run. There is a fated course of history which needs to be followed. Lenin and his friends are *bound* to win, he says. Dialectical necessity is on their side because they know about it and are its conscious representatives as agents in history.

But Lenin personally bends this necessity somewhat, because he does not take Marx's and Engels' views on material organization quite literally. Tsarist Russia is in the main respects feudalistic, having a large peasant population and only a small minority of industrial workers. Lenin nonetheless wants to conduct a "Marxist" revolution there. Yet from a Marxian viewpoint Tsarist Russia lacks the technological prerequisites for socialism and communism. It cannot produce enough goods. It has no super-machine yet.[1]

Why would socialism or communism have to wait for the emergence of the super-machine? Because capitalism is the great innovative force in modern history. Competition in capitalism leads to technological innovations because the only way to survive or flourish, as an investor in capitalism, is by continually finding more efficient productive technologies than your competitors. This is how Marx argues in *Capital*. Hence, if one leaps over the capitalistic phase then one will not be able to feed a socialistic society. The tools will be missing.

One should notice how deep this difference is. Marx and Engels are *materialists*, saying that changes in the productive relations always come first in history. Changes in ideas and class formations are only repercussions of the real material drama. In contrast, Lenin prioritizes political decisions. He believes a leap can be made in history by making decisions and acting on them effectively. (In other words, Lenin is a "Bolshevik," not an orthodox Marxist or "Menshevik." He believes in the organizational power of a vanguard party and not as much in the economy.)

This may at first sound like *Plato* (see Chapter 2). For Plato's Kallipolis is constructed by means of central planning. There is then not a material change first and then a mental one, as in Marx. Rather, the mental comes first. The mental change causes the material. This is the reverse of Marx. For the trained dialecticians in Plato rise to the Good and then turn back down, imposing their plans on the mundane city.

Yet, if one looks only a little more closely one notices that Lenin is not on Plato's side either, because he does not recognize anything like the Good. The independent authority of the Forms is a fiction for Lenin.

---

[1] Lenin's departure from Marx has drastic effects also because on this notable point *Stalin* follows Lenin. Under Stalin the Soviet Union industrializes by means of central planning. See Tucker Chapter 5 for discussion.

Also, Lenin has no time for lengthy dialectical proofs about principles. He is not about asking *Why...?* until this proves impossible. He wants action, not speculation. There is no time for all those questions. Lenin is not a materialist or an idealist but a "pragmatist." He assumes the validity of his ends and looks opportunistically for the most effective means to them. He is not concerned with anything like self-criticism or self-creation.

Mao first marches down the trail blazed by Engels and Lenin and then changes his course. The following excerpts are from *On Contradiction* (1937):

> The dialectical world outlook emerged in ancient times both in China and in Europe. Ancient dialectics, however, had a somewhat spontaneous and naive character; in the social and historical conditions then prevailing, it was not yet able to form a theoretical system, hence it could not fully explain the world and was supplanted by metaphysics. The famous German philosopher Hegel, who lived in the late 18th and early 19th centuries, made most important contributions to dialectics, but his dialectics was idealist. It was not until Marx and Engels, the great protagonists of the proletarian movement, had synthesized the positive achievements in the history of human knowledge and, in particular, critically absorbed the rational elements of Hegelian dialectics and created the great theory of dialectical and historical materialism that an unprecedented revolution occurred in the history of human knowledge. This theory was further developed by Lenin and Stalin. As soon as it spread to China, it wrought tremendous changes in the world of Chinese thought.

There is a simple reason why Mao would side with Lenin. He, like Lenin, wants to conduct a "Marxist" revolution in a backward, pre-industrialic region.[1]

But Mao adds his own twist to things:

> [...] the world outlook of materialist dialectics holds that in order to understand the development of a thing we should study it internally and in its relations with other things; in other words, the development of things should be seen as their internal and necessary self-movement, while each thing in its movement is interrelated with and interacts on the things around it. The fundamental cause of the development of a thing is not external but internal; it lies in the contradictoriness within the thing. There is internal contradiction in every single thing, hence its motion and development.

---

[1] This same problem repeats in many of the supposedly "Marxist" revolutions of the past century. They occur in poor countries, which lack the material basis for socialism and communism according to Marx and Engels. See Tucker Chapters 5–6 for discussion.

Contradictoriness within a thing is the fundamental cause of its development, while its interrelations and interactions with other things are secondary causes. Thus materialist dialectics effectively combats the theory of external causes, or of an external motive force, advanced by metaphysical mechanical materialism and vulgar evolutionism. It is evident that purely external causes can only give rise to mechanical motion, that is, to changes in scale or quantity, but cannot explain why things differ qualitatively in thousands of ways and why one thing changes into another. As a matter of fact, even mechanical motion under external force occurs through the internal contradictoriness of things. Simple growth in plants and animals, their quantitative development, is likewise chiefly the result of their internal contradictions. Similarly, social development is due chiefly not to external but to internal causes.

Like many "Marxists," Mao holds that dialectics operate according to iron laws. But his emphasis is on internal versus external dialectics. This emphasis has political implications:

> Countries with almost the same geographical and climatic conditions display great diversity and unevenness in their development. Moreover, great social changes may take place in one and the same country although its geography and climate remain unchanged. Imperialist Russia changed into the socialist Soviet Union, and feudal Japan, which had locked its doors against the world, changed into imperialist Japan, although no change occurred in the geography and climate of either country. Long dominated by feudalism, China has undergone great changes in the last hundred years and is now changing in the direction of a new China, liberated and free, and yet no change has occurred in her geography and climate. Changes do take place in the geography and climate of the earth as a whole and in every part of it, but they are insignificant when compared with changes in society; geographical and climatic changes manifest themselves in terms of tens of thousands of years, while social changes manifest themselves in thousands, hundreds or tens of years, and even in a few years or months in times of revolution. According to materialist dialectics, changes in nature are due chiefly to the development of the internal contradictions in nature. Changes in society are due chiefly to the development of the internal contradictions in society, that is, the contradiction between the productive forces and the relations of production, the contradiction between classes and the contradiction between the old and the new; it is the development of these contradictions that pushes society forward and gives the impetus for the supersession of the old society by the new. Does materialist dialectics exclude external causes? Not at all. It holds that external causes are the condition of change

and internal causes are the basis of change, and that external causes become operative through internal causes. In a suitable temperature an egg changes into a chicken, but no temperature can change a stone into a chicken, because each has a different basis.

The external forces do exist, but their effects are lesser. Climates, temperatures, foreign powers, etc., can affect things but they cannot cause fundamental changes.

What Mao wants ultimately to say is that China must follow its own special path:

> There is constant interaction between the peoples of different countries. In the era of capitalism, and especially in the era of imperialism and proletarian revolution, the interaction and mutual impact of different countries in the political, economic and cultural spheres are extremely great. The October Socialist Revolution ushered in a new epoch in world history as well as in Russian history. It exerted influence on internal changes in the other countries in the world and, similarly and in a particularly profound way, on internal changes in China. These changes, however, were effected through the inner laws of development of these countries, China included. In battle, one army is victorious and the other is defeated, both the victory and the defeat are determined by internal causes.

Finally, it is imperative that China is internally unified:

> The one is victorious either because it is strong or because of its competent generalship, the other is vanquished either because it is weak or because of its incompetent generalship; it is through internal causes that external causes become operative. In China in 1927, the defeat of the proletariat by the big bourgeoisie came about through the opportunism then to be found within the Chinese proletariat itself (inside the Chinese Communist Party). When we liquidated this opportunism, the Chinese revolution resumed its advance. Later, the Chinese revolution again suffered severe setbacks at the hands of the enemy, because adventurism had risen within our Party. When we liquidated this adventurism, our cause advanced once again. Thus it can be seen that to lead the revolution to victory, a political party must depend on the correctness of its own political line and the solidity of its own organization.

The internal unity of China can be preserved only by liquidating adventurists and opportunists! In other words, the Chinese must be brought to agree with each other. China has only one voice.

What really happens in history is that Mao himself takes the lead. It is he with whom the Chinese must agree. He is the chief architect not only in the communist revolution of China in 1949 but also in the

Great Leap Forward in 1957 and perhaps to some degree in the Cultural Revolution of 1966.[1]

Is Mao's view dialectical? Apparently he makes an arbitrary choice in viewing the nation or region of China as an independent unit. One might impose consistency on oneself by expressing oneself as an alienated individual or as a class, but to do so as a nation is not a Marxist option. Moreover, harmony should always be *self*-imposed in a dialectic, but Mao forces things through, imposing his will on a billion others. He is not careful to assess whether what he wants actually accords with the needs and talents of the people.

Further Reading

Friedrich Engels: *Anti-Dühring.* Engels discusses many topics in plain language, in general taking views that are very different from this book's.

Erich Fromm: *Marx's Concept of Man.* This is a simplified account that is easy for beginners to approach.

Karl Marx: *Works.* As always, the original classics are the most stimulating to read.

Robert Tucker: *The Marxist Revolutionary Idea.* This is a clear introduction with a strong thesis of its own.

(See the Bibliography at the end of this book for detailed information on these and other titles.)

---

[1] See Chang and Halliday, and Carter.

Appendix A. Popper

Karl Popper (1902–1994) is a, if not the, major recent critic of dialectics. He objects to the dialecticians Plato, Hegel, and Marx in his *The Open Society and its Enemies* in 1945, blaming them for pretending to justify the totalitarian social orders of the right as well as the left. Popper says that dialectical thinking is to blame for the extremism and dystopianism of the Fascists, of the Third Reich, and of the Soviet Union. So many horrors of the past century are due to the irrationality of the dialecticians, from world wars and mass starvation to persecution and intolerance. Of course, accusations cannot get more radical than this. Popper is giving dialectic a very bad name.

Why does Popper do this? He explains:

> This book [...] sketches some of the difficulties faced by our civilization — a civilization which might be perhaps described as aiming at humaneness and reasonableness, at equality and freedom; a civilization which is still in its infancy, as it were, and which continues to grow in spite of the fact that it has been so often betrayed by so many of the intellectual leaders of mankind. It attempts to show that this civilization has not yet fully recovered from the shock of its birth — the transition from the tribal or 'closed society', with its submission to magical forces, to the 'open society' which sets free the critical powers of man. It attempts to show that the shock of this transition is one of the factors that have made possible the rise of those reactionary movements which have tried, and still try, to overthrow civilization and to return to tribalism. And it suggests that what we call nowadays totalitarianism belongs to a tradition which is just as old or just as young as our civilization itself.

It tries thereby to contribute to our understanding of totalitarianism, and of the significance of the perennial fight against it.[1]

Popper has just said that there is a conflict between "closed" and "open" models of society. Totalitarians leap backwards to the closed alternative because the open one proves to be too much for them.

Popper continues:

> It further tries to examine the application of the critical and rational methods of science to the problems of the open society. It analyses the principles of democratic social reconstruction, the principles of what I may term 'piecemeal social engineering' in opposition to 'Utopian social engineering' (as explained in Chapter 9). And it tries to clear away some of the obstacles impeding a rational approach to the problems of social reconstruction. It does so by criticizing those social philosophies which are responsible for the widespread prejudice against the possibilities of democratic reform.[2]

Popper is for openness and hence also for piecemeal social engineering. The advocates of the closed alternative are for utopian social engineering. What is the difference between the piecemeal and utopian alternatives? The utopian alternative is much more ambitious:

> I use the name methodological essentialism to characterize the view, held by Plato and many of his followers, that it is the task of pure knowledge or "science" to discover and to describe the true nature of things, i.e., their hidden reality or essence. It was Plato's peculiar belief that the essence of sensible things can be found in other and more real things — in their primogenitors or Forms. Many of the later methodological essentialists, for instance Aristotle, did not altogether follow him in this; but they all agreed with him in determining the task of pure knowledge as the discovery of the hidden nature or Form or essence of things. All these methodological essentialists also agreed with Plato in holding that these essences may be discovered and discerned with the help of intellectual intuition; that every essence has a name proper to it, the name after which the sensible things are called; and that it may be described in words. And a description of the essence of a thing they all called a "definition." According to methodological essentialism, there can be three ways of knowing a thing: I mean that we can know its unchanging reality or essence; and that we can know the definition of the essence; and that we can know its name. Accordingly, two questions may be formulated about any real thing . . . : A person may give the name and ask for the definition; or he may give the definition and ask for the "name." As an example of this method, Plato uses

---

[1] *Open Society* Vol. 1, Introduction.
[2] *Open Society* Vol. 1, Chapter 3, section 6.

the essence of "even" (as opposed to "odd"): "Number" . . . may be a thing capable of division into equal parts. If it is so divisible, number is named "even"; and the definition of the name "even" is "a number divisible into equal parts." . . And when we are given the name and asked about the definition, or when we are given the definition and asked about the name, we speak, in both cases, of one and the same essence, whether we call it now "even" or "a number divisible into equal parts."' After this example, Plato proceeds to apply this method to a 'proof concerning the real nature of the soul, about which we shall hear more later.

Methodological essentialism, i.e., the theory that it is the aim of science to reveal essences and to describe them by means of definitions, can be better understood when contrasted with its opposite, methodological nominalism. Instead of aiming at finding out what a thing really is, and at defining its true nature, methodological nominalism aims at describing how a thing behaves in various circumstances, and especially, whether there are any regularities in its behavior. In other words, methodological nominalism sees the aim of science in the description of the things and events of our experience, and in an 'explanation' of these events, i.e., their description with the help of universal laws. And it sees in our language, and especially in those of its rules which distinguish properly constructed sentences and inferences from a mere heap of words, the great instrument of scientific description; words it considers rather as subsidiary tools for this task, and not as names of essences. The methodological nominalist will never think that a question like "What is energy?" or "What is movement?" or "What is an atom?" is an important question for physics; but he will attach importance to a question like: "How can the energy of the sun be made useful?" or "How does a planet move?" or "Under what condition does an atom radiate light?" And to those philosophers who tell him that before having answered the "what is" question he cannot hope to give exact answers to any of the "how" questions, he will reply, if at all, by pointing out that he much prefers that modest degree of exactness which he can achieve by his methods to the pretentious muddle which they have achieved by theirs.

As indicated by our example, methodological nominalism is nowadays fairly generally accepted in the natural sciences. The problems of the social sciences, on the other hand, are still for the most part treated by essentialist methods. This is, in my opinion, one of the main reasons for their backwardness. But many who have noticed this situation judge it differently. They believe that the difference in method is necessary, and that it reflects an 'essential' difference between the 'natures' of these two fields of research.[1]

Methodological essentialists have ambitious goals for their research. They want to identify things as they really are, in themselves. Unlike methodological nominalists they will not settle for mere predictability in experiences. They want more — too much, says Popper. They have become rare in the natural sciences but in the social sciences they still exist.

All that one can rationally expect to find out about things is, Popper means, what experiences come after what. You see a certain quantity of a chemical compound somewhere, plus a certain quantity of another chemical compound (in certain conditions), and chemistry can tell you what will happen. Why can it? Because chemists have experimented with the same combination enough times. Now they feel they can generalize that it is a scientific law that the same thing will always happen. They have tested the combination so many times. But they admit, just like piecemeal engineers, that the results could turn out to be different any day. That is just what makes them "open." They are open in being open to news. For Popper all scientists are like this, and this may well be correct.[2]

In another work, *The Logic of Scientific Discovery*, Popper argues that scientific theories are distinct from other views in being falsifiable. They are risky. Science is risky. In contrast, myths are safe, because no evidence can count against them. Why not? Because myths are not clear about what they mean to predict. Consequently their falsifiers are inexistent or obscure. They are unscientific because they are immune to empirical criticism. That is what is wrong with dialectics according to Popper. Plato seems to aim high, and he seems to reason, but the fact is that we do not even know how we might measure whether he is right or not. This is because we cannot get clear on just what he means to predict. Similarly for Hegel and Marx. They do not expose themselves to criticism. That is how they are "closed."

Popper emphasizes that this is not to accuse Socrates of anything:

> Socrates had stressed that he was not wise; that he was not in the possession of truth, but that he was a searcher, an inquirer, a lover of truth. This, he explained, is expressed by the word "philosopher," i.e., the lover of wisdom, and the seeker for it, as opposed to "Sophist," i.e., the professionally wise man. If ever he claimed that statesmen should be philosophers, he could only have meant that, burdened

---

[1] Ibid.
[2] But there have been critics, e.g., Putnam.

with an excessive responsibility, they should be searchers for truth, and conscious of their limitations.[1]

Socrates is a long way from Plato:

> How did Plato convert this doctrine? At first sight, it might appear that he did not alter it at all, when demanding that the sovereignty of the state should be invested in the philosophers; especially since, like Socrates, he defined philosophers as lovers of truth. But the change made by Plato is indeed tremendous. His lover is no longer the modest seeker, he is the proud possessor of truth. A trained dialectician, he is capable of intellectual intuition, i.e., of seeing, and of communicating with, the eternal, the heavenly Forms or Ideas. Placed high above all ordinary men, he is 'god-like, if not .. divine', both in his wisdom and in his power. Plato's ideal philosopher approaches both to omniscience and to omnipotence. He is the Philosopher-King. It is hard, I think, to conceive a greater contrast than that between the Socratic and the Platonic ideal of a philosopher. It is the contrast between two worlds — the world of a modest, rational individualist and that of a totalitarian demi-god.[2]

Popper is not altogether misled about the difference between Socrates and Plato: Chapter 2 said some similar things. Plato answers while Socrates asks.

But there are a few things that Popper overlooks which make one suspect that he is rather dramatically mistaken.

First, something about Socrates. Socrates certainly sought definitions that were more than nominal. He was after essences. Even more, he examined values and not facts, which is something a naturalist like Popper is barred from doing (because he is confined to empirical observations as standards of truth). Still more, Socrates was after something quite utopian, namely self-knowledge. He placed his standards high. That is why he was so dissatisfied with the Athens of his time. If he had been only an open-minded man he would have kept on asking questions without any special principles, that is without developing his self-predicated aims or his idealistic rhetoric of the gadfly. If Socrates had been Popperian then he would have been happy in Athens, but he was unhappy. Socrates is the man who died for the sake of the examined life. But he did not die for methodological nominalism, and probably no sane person would.

Second, something about piecemeal and utopian engineers. If things are largely well in a society, or in a branch of inquiry, then one may maintain that fair criticisms regarding it must be moderate and not

---

[1] *Open Society* Vol. 1, Chapter 7, Section 4.
[2] Ibid.

radical. But if things are badly then it would be misleading to claim that one is on the side of the just and the fair as a *moderate*. For instance, Martin Luther King Jr.'s views and actions were in some ways radical, and they questioned the values of King's environment in the American South. King was not content to do empirical studies and to wait for gradual change. But hence Popper would have consistently sided *against* King. King invoked principles and required sweeping changes immediately. But this makes King a "closed" man, a man with a strong program and without any potential falsifiers to compromise with. And yet this is not an implication of his position which Popper makes obvious. (The implication is called *conservatism*.) In the meantime, a dialectician could easily side *with* King. In this book we have found values in Socrates, Kant, and Marx that could be used against the hostile environment that King faced in the American South and against Popper. For we have studied Socrates' questions to everyone about ends, Kant's Categorical Imperative, and Marx on the need of human self-expression. Notice that these are radical values that Popper's scientists do not exemplify or thematize in doing science. Moreover, they are *not* falsifiable empirically. Popper should be against them. To this background, Popper may not be as anti-totalitarian as he thinks he is. Perhaps he has sought out the wrong villains and the wrong heroes. For it seems that his villains should not be the dialecticians and that his heroes should not be the scientists.[1] (Now see Appendix B.)

---

[1] For discussions on Popper see Keuth and Ackermann.

Appendix B. The Frankfurt School

The Frankfurt School is a recent source of dialectical insights. Its members tend to express themselves in fragments, not in systems. The more original minds among them seem to be especially difficult to understand. Walter Benjamin is perhaps the most cryptic and the most novel. Yet some members of the same school have also been more accessible. Perhaps the easiest to approach is Herbert Marcuse (1898–1979). Marcuse adopts many of the ideas of Horkheimer and Adorno, who in certain ways follow Benjamin (as well as outsiders to the school like Lukacs, Weber, and Marx).[1] Marcuse is not as novel a mind as these others but he is more transparent, so let us take him as our guide in this short appendix.

Marcuse formulates a position that differs radically from Popper's. He says:

> The technological processes of mechanization and standardization might release individual energy into a yet uncharted realm of freedom beyond necessity. The very structure of human existence would be altered; the individual would be liberated from the work world's imposing upon him alien needs and alien possibilities. The individual would be free to exert autonomy over a life that would be his own. If the productive apparatus could be organized and directed toward the satisfaction of the vital needs, its control might well be centralized; such control would not prevent individual autonomy, but render it possible.

> This is a goal within the capabilities of advanced industrial civilization, the "end" of technological rationality. In actual fact, however, the contrary trend operates: the apparatus imposes its economic and

---

[1] See Buck-Morss and Jay on the complex history.

political requirements for defense and expansion on labor time and free time, on the material and intellectual culture. By virtue of the way it has organized its technological base, contemporary industrial society tends to be totalitarian. For "totalitarian" is not only a terroristic political coordination of society, but also a non-terroristic economic-technical coordination which operates through the manipulation of needs by vested interests. It thus precludes the emergence of an effective opposition against the whole. Not only a specific form of government or party rule makes for totalitarianism, but also a specific system of production and distribution [...].[1]

Marcuse first outlines the old and familiar Marxian dream that humans should be free while machines do their work for them. But then, in the next paragraph, he notes why this is not actually the utopia that is being set up in Western societies. Many are not even aiming at it. They want something else. What is that?

Society reproduced itself in a growing technical ensemble of things and relations which included the technical utilization of men—in other words, the struggle for existence and the exploitation of man and nature became ever more' scientific and rational. The double meaning of "rationalization" is relevant in this context. Scientific management and scientific division of labor vastly increased the productivity: of the economic, political, and cultural enterprise.[2]

The very purpose of modern societies has become technocratic. One seeks to manipulate one's surroundings simply to experience power. One wants, as it were, to be the controlling machine among other machines.

Who can enjoy such a thing, or value it as an end? Is Marcuse's generalization about contemporary society not too absurd to be believed? Can anyone sincerely think like Marcuse's technocrat?[3] Marcuse concedes that consciously thinking in this way may actually be rare in modern Western societies:

The distinguishing feature of advanced industrial society is its effective suffocation of those needs which demand liberation — liberation also from that which is tolerable and rewarding and

---

[1] From *One-Dimensional Man*, Part 1, Chapter 1.
[2] From *One-Dimensional Man*, Part 2, Chapter 6.
[3] Of course, this question would not sound so odd to Thrasymachus, Callicles, Hobbes, or Nietzsche, for whom it is normal for agents to seek power for its own sake (see Chapter 2).
The Frankfurt School's studies of "authoritarian personalities" are relevant here. Perhaps the best known is *The Authoritarian Personality* by Adorno and others (see Bibliography).

comfortable — while it sustains and absolves the destructive power and repressive function of the affluent society. Here, the social controls exact the overwhelming need for the production and consumption of waste; the need for stupefying work where it is no longer a real necessity; the need for modes of relaxation which soothe and prolong this stupefaction; the need for maintaining such deceptive liberties as free competition at administered prices, a free press which censors itself, free choice between brands and gadgets.[1]

The work most people do stupefies, and so does the entertainment that is usually consumed. Consequently people's horizons get clouded. All the while there is an illusion of freedom, and this illusion is what individuals tend to cling to:

> Under the rule of a repressive whole, liberty can be made into a powerful instrument of domination. The range of choice open to the individual is not the decisive factor in determining the degree of human freedom, but *what* can be chosen and what is chosen by the individual. The criterion for free choice can never be an absolute one, but neither is it entirely relative. Free election of masters does not abolish the masters or the slaves. Free choice among a wide variety of goods and services does not signify freedom if these goods and services sustain social controls over a life of toil and fear—that is, if they sustain alienation. And the spontaneous reproduction of superimposed needs by the individual does not establish autonomy; it only testifies to the efficacy of the controls.[2] (Italics in original.)

Small choices are hyped up so that one is fooled into thinking that one gets to make important decisions. One does not know to be dissatisfied.

But the philosophies which predominate do not even view this as demeaning. It is said to be only normal, for all cognitive processes:

> The quantification of nature, which led to its explication in terms of mathematical structures, separated reality from all inherent ends and, consequently, separated the true from the good, science from ethics. [...] Outside this rationality, one lives in a world of values, and values separated out from the objective reality become subjective.[...]

> Made into a methodological principle, this suspension has a twofold consequence: (a) it strengthens the shift of theoretical emphasis from the metaphysical "What is . . . ?" to the functional "How . . . ?," and (b) it establishes a practical (though by no

---

[1] From *One-Dimensional Man*, Part 1, Chapter 1.
[2] Ibid.

means absolute) certainty which, in its operations with matter, is with good conscience free from commitment to any substance outside the operational context. In other words, theoretically, the transformation of man and nature has no other objective limits than those offered by the brute factuality of matter, its still unmastered resistance to knowledge and control. To the degree to which this conception becomes applicable and effective in reality, the latter is approached as a (hypothetical) system of instrumentalities; the metaphysical "being-as-such" gives way to "being-instrument." Moreover, proved in its effectiveness, this conception works as an *a priori*—*it* predetermines experience, it *projects* the direction of the transformation of nature, it organizes the whole.[1] (Italics in original.)

The technocratic order, which is not interested in a liberating utopia, has a pragmatic conception of reality and knowledge. According to its philosophy things do not have their own characteristics independently of us. Things are known or real only when they are useful. Useful for what? For whatever values that happen to predominate. For the instrumentalists' *aims* cannot be rationally evaluated. Only means are subject to rational control. Usefulness or efficiency is the only standard of criticism and progress.

Notice that the thinking that Marcuse is here blaming for a quasi-totalitarian social order is strikingly close to *Popper's*. From Marcuse's angle Popper has matters upside down. It is not dialectical thinking that is to blame for totalitarian organizations, and it is not piecemeal engineering that liberates one from totalitarianism. Rather, things are the other way around. It is the piecemeal pragmatism that gets one *into* totalitarianism in the first place. (The Nazis were *proud* of having values that could not be rationally assessed. They *loved* power, purely for its own sake.) Dialectic would take us *out* of dystopia, not into it. How is this? It transcends the limits of actual existence:

> [C]ritical philosophic thought is necessarily transcendent and *abstract*. Philosophy shares this abstractness with all genuine thought, for nobody really thinks who does not abstract from that which is given, who does not relate the facts to the factors which have made them, who does not—in his mind—undo the facts. Abstractness is the very life of thought, the token of its authenticity.[2] (Italics in original.)

---

[1] From *One-Dimensional Man*, Part 2, Chapter 6.
[2] From *One-Dimensional Man*, Part 1, Chapter 1.

Dialectical thought is not about adapting to whatever happens to be one's environment. Rather it is about stepping over such limits, with creative freedom:

> The philosophic quest proceeds from the finite world to the construction of a reality which is not subject to the painful difference between potentiality and actuality, which has mastered its negativity and—is complete and independent in itself—free.[1]

How is thinking of this kind possible? Marcuse explains that in Plato's dialectic,

> the terms "Being" "Non-being" "Movement," "the One and the Many" "Identity" and "Contradiction" are methodically kept open, ambiguous, not fully defined. They have an open horizon, an entire universe of meaning which is gradually structured in the process of communication itself, but which is never closed. The propositions are submitted, developed, and tested in a dialogue, in which the partner is led to question the normally unquestioned universe of experience and speech, and to enter a new dimension of discourse— otherwise he is *free* and the discourse is addressed to his freedom. He is supposed to go beyond that which is given to him—as the speaker, in his proposition, goes beyond the initial setting of the terms. These terms have many meanings because the conditions to which they refer have many sides, implications, and effects which cannot be insulated and stabilized. Their logical development responds to the process of reality, or *Sache selbst*. The laws of thought are laws of reality, or rather *become* the laws of reality if thought understands the truth of immediate experience as the appearance of another truth, which is that of the true Forms of reality—of the Ideas. Thus there is contradiction rather than correspondence between dialectical thought and the given reality [...].[2] (Italics in original.)

What opens up the possibilities for dialectics or free thoughts is the unsettled character of the terms and topics that they concern. To use an example that was used earlier in this book, if the character of meaning is not obvious then it becomes possible to say new and penetrating things about meaning. Conversely, if meaning is only what everyday speech makes it out to be, or if it has already been determined by positive science, then no one can say anything new or deep about it. It needs to be *beyond* the range of our present habits to qualify as an object of free minds or we can look forward only to piecemeal revisions

---

[1] From *One-Dimensional Man*, Part 2, Chapter 6.
[2] Ibid.

at most and say good-bye to any meaningful degree of freedom. For this *beyond* gives us some space to move around in. But Marcuse is saying that dialectical terms are just like this. They are *not yet* defined but they are *to be* defined. That is why dialectics link so nicely with freedom.[1]

---

[1] Actually, it is not perfectly clear that Marcuse and the other Frankfurt theorists agree with this positive aim. They may not want definitions, determinate self-relations, or the like. For their dialectics tend to be negative, consisting of many problems and few solutions (see Buck-Morss and Jay for discussion). In this way their negative dialectics are unlike the dialectics of Socrates, Kant, and Marx.

But nonetheless I want to suggest that the dialectics of Marcuse and the rest of the Frankfurt School are closer to being true to the tradition of freedom and criticism that so many Western authors trace back to Socrates.

BIBLIOGRAPHY

Ackermann, Robert John. *The Philosophy of Karl Popper*. Cambridge, Mass.: University of Massachusetts Press, 1976.

Adorno, Theodor W., Else Frenkel-Brunswik, Daniel Levinson and Nevitt Sanford. *The Authoritarian Personality, Studies in Prejudice Series*, Volume 1. New York: Harper & Row, 1950.

Allison, Henry A. *Kant's Transcendental Idealism: An Interpretation and Defense*. New Haven: Yale University press, 2004.

Aristotle. *The Works of Aristotle*, 2 Vols., transl. W.D. Ross. London: Britannica, 1952.

Arpaly, Nomy. "Which Autonomy?" reprinted in Campbell et. al., eds., pp. 173-188.

Barnes, Jonathan. *The Pre-Socratic Philosophers*. London: Routledge, 1983.

Beets, M.G.J. *Socrates on Death and the Beyond: A Companion to Plato's Phaedo*. Amsterdam: Duna, 1997.

Beiser, Frederick C. *German Idealism: The Struggle against Subjectivism, 1781-1801*. Cambridge, Mass.: Harvard University Press, 2002.

Bernstein, Eduard. *Evolutionary Socialism: A Criticism and Affirmation*, transl. Edith C. Harvey. London: Independent Labour Party, 1907.

Beversluis, John. *Cross-Examining Socrates: A Defense of the Interlocutors in Plato's Early Dialogues*. Cambridge: Cambridge University Press, 2000.

Bhaskar, Roy. *Dialectic: The Pulse of Freedom*. London: Routledge, 2008.

BonJour, Laurence. "The Dialectic of Foundationalism and Coherentism," in John Greco and Ernest Sosa, eds., pp. 117-141.

Bostock, David. *Aristotle, Zeno, and the Potential Infinite.* London: Aristotelian Society, 1972.

Bostock, David. *Plato's Phaedo.* Oxford: Oxford University Press, 1986.

Buck-Morss, Susan. *The Origin of Negative Dialectics:* Theodor W. Adorno, Walter Benjamin, and the Frankfurt Institute. New York: Free Press, 1977.

Campbell, Joseph Keim, O'Rourke, Michael, and Shier, David, eds. *Freedom and Determinism.* Cambridge, Mass.: MIT Press, 2004.

Carter, Peter. *Mao.* Oxford: Oxford University Press, 1976.

Chang, Jung and Halliday, Jon. *Mao: The Unknown Story.* London: Jonathan Cape, 2005.

Chomsky, Noam. *The Knowledge of Language: Its Nature, Origins, and Use.* New York: Praeger, 1986.

Culler, Jonathan. *Structuralist Poetics: Structuralism, Linguistics, and the Study of Literature.* London: Routledge & Kegan Paul, 1975.

Curd, Patricia. *The Legacy of Parmenides.* Princeton: Princeton University Press, 1997.

Descartes, Rene. *Meditations on First Philosophy,* transl. Donald A. Cress. Indianapolis: Hackett, 1993.

Edgerton, Franklin. *The Beginnings of Indian Philosophy.* London: George Allen and Unwin, 1965.

Fine, Gail, ed. *Plato,* 2 Vols. Oxford: Oxford University Press, 2000.

Fodor, Jerry A. and Lepore, Ernest. *The Compositionality Papers.* Oxford: Oxford University Press, 2002.

Fränkel, Hermann. "A Thought Pattern in Heraclitus," reprinted in Alexander Mourelatos, ed., pp. 214-228.

Frege, Gottlob. "On Sense and Reference," transl. M. Black in *Translations from the Philosophical Writings of Gottlob Frege,* P. Geach and M. Black, eds. and transl., pp. 25-50.

Fromm, Erich. *Marx's Concept of Man.* New York: Frederick Ungar, 1961.

Geach, Peter, and Black, Max, eds. and transl. *Translations from the Philosophical Writings of Gottlob Frege, 3rd Ed.* Oxford: Blackwell, third edition, 1980.

Greco, John, and Sosa, Ernest, eds. *The Blackwell Guide to Epistemology.* Oxford: Blackwell, 1999.

Greene, Brian. *The Elegant Universe: Superstrings, Hidden Dimensions, and the Quest for the Ultimate Theory.* New York: Norton & Company, 1999.

Habermas, Jürgen. *The Theory of Communicative Action*, 2 Vols. Boston: Beacon, 1985.

Hanhijärvi, Tommi Juhani. *Socrates' Criteria: A Libertarian Interpretation.* Lanham: University Press of America, 2012.

Hansen, Chad. *A Daoist Theory of Chinese Thought: A Philosophical Interpretation.* Oxford: Oxford University Press, 2000.

Hegel, Georg Wilhelm Friedrich. *Hegel's Science of Logic*, transl. A. V. Miller. New Work: Prometheus, 1991.

Horstmann, Rolf-Peter. *Ontologie und Relationen: Hegel, Bradley, Russell und die Kontroverse über interne und externe Beziehungen.* Hain: Königstein, 1984.

Jaeger, Werner. *Paideia*, 3 Vols., transl. Gilbert Highet. Oxford: Oxford University Press, 1944.

Jaspers, Karl. *The Origin and Goal of History.* transl. Michael Bullock. New Haven, CT: Yale University Press, 1953.

Jaspers, Karl. *Reason and Existenz.* transl. William Earle. New York: Noonday Press, 1955.

Jay, Martin. *The Dialectical Imagination:* A History of the Frankfurt School and the Institute of Social Research, 1923-1950. Berkeley: University of California Press, 1973.

Jubien, Michael. *Contemporary Metaphysics:* An Introduction. London: Blackwell, 1997.

Jung, Carl Gustav. *The Archetypes and the Collective Unconscious*, transl. R.F.C. Hull. Princeton: Princeton University Press, 1969.

Kant, Immanuel. *Critique of Judgment*, transl. J. H. Bernard. London: Macmillan, 1892.

Kant, Immanuel. *Critique of Pure Reason*, transl. John Miller Dow Meiklejohn. New York: Prometheus, 1991.

Kant, Immanuel. *Fundamental Principles of the Metaphysic of Morals*, transl. Thomas Kingsmill Abbott. London: Longmans, Green & Co, 1895.

Katz, Jerrold. *Language & Other Abstract Objects.* Lanham: Rowman & Littlefield, 1980.

Kenny, Anthony. *Descartes: A Study of His Philosophy.* New York: Random House, 1968.

Keuth, Herbert. *The Philosophy of Karl Popper.* Cambridge: Cambridge University Press, 2004.

Kierkegaard, Søren. *Philosophical Fragments*, transl. Edna H. Hong and Howard V. Hong. Princeton: Princeton University Press, 1985.

Kolakowski, Leszek. *Main Currents of Marxism*, 3 Vols., transl. P.S. Falla. Oxford: Clarendon Press, 1978.

Krämer, Hans Joachim, and Catan, John R., eds. *Plato and the Foundations of Metaphysics: A Work on the Theory of the Principles and Unwritten Doctrines of Plato with a Collection of the Fundamental Documents.* Albany: State University of New York Press, 1990.

Legge, J., ed. Sacred Books of the East, Vol. 39. Oxford: Oxford University Press, 1891.

Lenin, Vladimir Ilyich. *Collected Works*, Vol. 7, transl. Abraham Fineberg and Naomi Jochel. Moscow: Progress Publishers, 1964.

Magnus, Bernd. *Nietzsche's Existential Imperative.* Indianapolis: University of Indiana Press, 1978.

Manuel, Frank E. and Manuel, Fritzie P. *Utopian Thought in the Western World.* Cambridge, Mass.: Belknap Press, 1982.

Mao, Zedong. *On Contradiction.* Beijing: Foreign Language Press, 1965.

Marcuse, Herbert. *One-Dimensional Man.* Boston: Beacon, 1964.

Marcuse, Herbert. *Reason and Revolution: Hegel and the Rise of Social Theory.* Boston: Beacon, 1968.

Marx, Karl and Engels, Friedrich. *Collected Works.* London: Lawrence and Wishart, 2005.

Mourelatos, Alexander, ed. *The Pre-Socratics: A Collection of Critical Essays.* Princeton: Princeton University Press, 1994.

Nehamas, Alexander. "Self-Predication and Plato's Theory of Forms." *American Philosophical Quarterly*, Vol. 16, Number 2.

Nietzsche, Friedrich. *The Birth of Tragedy: Out of the Spirit of Music*, transl. Shaun Whiteside. London: Penguin, 1994.

Paramananda, Swami, ed. *The Upanishads.* Frankfurt: Aeterna, 2010.

Penner, Terry. *The Ascent from Nominalism: Some Existence Arguments in Plato's Middle Dialogues.* New York: Springer, 1987.

Plato: *The Complete Works of Plato*, transl. Benjamin Jowett. New York: Scribner's, 1871.

Popper, Karl. *Conjectures and Refutations:* The Growth of Scientific Knowledge. London: Routledge, 1963.

Popper, Karl. *The Logic of Scientific Discovery.* London: Routledge, 1959.

Popper, Karl. *The Open Society and its Enemies*, 2 Vols., 5th Ed. Princeton: Princeton University Press, 1971.

Prior, William. *Virtue and Knowledge: An Introduction to Ancient Greek Ethics.* London: Routledge, 1991.

Putnam, Hilary. "The Corroboration of Theories," reprinted in Hilary Putnam, pp. 250-269.

Putnam, Hilary. *Philosophical Papers*, Vol. 1. Cambridge: Cambridge University Press, 1975.

Reeve, C.D.C. *Philosopher-Kings: The Argument of Plato's Republic*. Indianapolis: Hackett, 2006.

Russell, Bertrand. "Mathematics and the Metaphysicians," in *Mysticism and Logic*, pp. 74-96.

Russell, Bertrand. *Mysticism and Logic and Other Essays*. London: Allen & Unwin, 1918.

Russell, Bertrand. *The Principles of Mathematics*. Cambridge: Cambridge University Press, 1903.

Santas, Gerasimos Xenophon. *Socrates*. London: Routledge, 1983.

Sassoon, Donald. *One Hundred Years of Socialism: The West European Left in the Twentieth Century*. New York: Tauris, 1996.

Silverman, Allan: *The Dialectic of Essence: A Study of Plato's Metaphysics*. Princeton: Princeton University Press, 2003.

Snell, Bruno. *The Discovery of the Mind: The Greek Origins of European Thought*, transl. T.G. Rosenmeyer. London: Blackwell, 1953.

Tannery, Paul. *Pour l'histoire de la science Hellène*. Paris: F. Alcan, 1887.

Taylor, A.E. *Plato: The Man and His Work*. London: Methuen, 1926.

Taylor, Charles. *Hegel*. Cambridge: Cambridge University Press, 1975.

Tucker, Robert C. *The Marxist Revolutionary Idea*. New York: Norton, 1969.

Vlastos, Gregory. *Socrates: Ironist and Moral Philosopher*. Ithaca: Cornell University Press, 1991.

Watts, Alan. *The Way of Zen*. New York: Random House, 1957.

Wittgenstein, Ludwig. *Philosophical Investigations*, transl. G.E.M. Anscombe, 2nd Ed. London: Basil Blackwell, 1968.

Zaehner, R.C. *Hinduism*. Oxford: Oxford University Press, 1962.

NAMES INDEX

Printed in the United States
By Bookmasters